81690

COLLIN COUNTY COMMUNITY COLLEGE

3 1702 00181 9154

Learning Resources Center
Collin County Community College District
SPRING CREEK CAMPUS
Plano, Texas   75074

WITHDRAWN

D0073077

Belarus

Postcommunist States and Nations

Books in the series

Belarus: a denationalized nation
David R. Marples

Armenia: at the crossroads
Joseph R. Masih and Robert O. Krikorian

Poland: the conquest of history
George Sanford

Kyrgyzstan: central asia's island of democracy?
John Anderson

This book is part of a series. The publisher will accept continuation orders which may be cancelled at any time and which provide for automatic billing and shipping of each title in the series upon publication. Please write for details.

Belarus

A DENATIONALIZED NATION

David R. Marples

harwood academic publishers
Australia • Canada • China • France
Germany • India • Japan • Luxembourg • Malaysia
The Netherlands • Russia • Singapore • Switzerland

Copyright © 1999 OPA (Overseas Publishers Association) N.V. Published by license under the Harwood Academic Publishers imprint, part of The Gordon and Breach Publishing Group.

All rights reserved.

No part of this book may be reproduced or utilized in any form or by any means, electronic or mechanical, including photocopying and recording, or by any information storage or retrieval system, without permission in writing from the publisher. Printed in Singapore.

Amsteldijk 166
1st Floor
1079 LH Amsterdam
The Netherlands

British Library Cataloguing in Publication Data

Marples, David R.
  Belarus: a denationalized nation. – (Postcommunist states & nations; v. 1)
  1. Belarus – History   2. Belarus – Economic conditions
  3. Belarus – Politics and government   4. Belarus – Foreign relations – Russia (Federation)   5. Russia (Federation) – Foreign relations – Belarus
  I. Title
  947.8′086

ISBN   90-5702-343-1 (softcover)
ISSN   1028-043X

FOR YULIA SHIMKO

TABLE OF CONTENTS

Chronology | ix

Preface | xi

Map of Belarus | xv

1 History of Belarus to 1985 | 1

2 The Economy: 1986–1996 | 27

3 Perestroyka and Independence, 1985–1993 | 47

4 A New Presidency, June 1994–Spring 1996 | 69

5 Lukashenka's Consolidation of Power | 89

6 Relations with Russia | 107

Bibliography | 129

Index | 131

CHRONOLOGY

862	Polatsk region is mentioned for the first time in the Primary Chronicle.
988	Kievan Rus' ruler Volodymyr accepts Christianity.
1263	Belarusian lands are incorporated into the Grand Duchy of Lithuania.
1385	Lithuania and Poland are united through marital ties of their rulers.
1529	Code of Laws of the Grand Duchy of Lithuania approved.
1569	Formation of a Polish-Lithuanian Commonwealth.
1596	A Uniate (Greek Catholic Church) is founded in the Grand Duchy of Lithuania at the Council of Brest.
1772–1795	Three Partitions of Poland between Austria, Russia and Prussia; all Belarusian territories are incorporated into the Russian Empire.
1863–1864	Polish rebellion against the Russian Empire with the participation of the Belarusian Kastus Kalinouski.
1914	Outbreak of World War I.
1917	Revolutions in Russia.
1918	Declaration of independence by the Belarusian Rada.
1919	A Soviet regime is declared in Belarus.
1 February– 18 July 1919	Existence of a Lithuanian-Belarusian Soviet regime.
1919–March 1921	Polish-Soviet war.
18 March 1921	Treaty of Riga ends Polish-Soviet war. Western Belarus is incorporated into Poland.
30 December 1922	Belarus becomes a member of the Union of Soviet Socialist Republics (USSR).
11 April 1927	A new Constitution is established for the BSSR.
1929–1932	Mass collectivization campaign in the BSSR.
1937–1941	Period of Stalin purges. Executions by the NKVD at Kurapaty, near Minsk.
17 September 1939	Soviet army invades Polish eastern territories.
October– December 1939	Formal incorporation of Western Belarus into the Soviet Union as part of the BSSR.
22 June 1941	Nazi Germany invades the Soviet Union.
1941–1944	Period of German occupation of Belarus.
3 July 1944	City of Minsk is recaptured by the Red Army.
1947–1948	Period of renewed repressions under guidance of Andrey Zhdanov.
1956–1965	Period of leadership of the 'Partisans' begins, when Kiryl T. Mazurau becomes the party leader.
1965–1980	Pyotr Masherau leads the Communist Party of Belarus.
26 April 1986	Accident at the Chernobyl nuclear power station in Ukraine severely contaminates Belarusian territory.
24–25 June 1989	Founding Congress of the Belarusian Popular Front in Vilnius, Lithuania.

23 June 1990	Vyachaslau Kebich is appointed Prime Minister of the BSSR.
27 July 1990	Belarus declares state sovereignty.
25 August 1991	Belarus declares independence in response to the failed putsch in Moscow.
19 September 1991	The BSSR is renamed the Republic of Belarus, with a new flag and state symbols.
19 September 1991	Stanislau Shushkevich is elected Speaker of the Supreme Soviet (parliament) of Belarus.
8 December 1991	The Belavezha agreement is signed between Russia, Ukraine and Belarus, forming the Commonwealth of Independent States (CIS).
25 December 1991	The Soviet Union is formally dissolved.
February 1993	The Belarusian parliament ratifies the START-1 Treaty and accepts the Nonproliferation Treaty as a neutral country.
May 1993	The Belarusian Popular Front forms a political party.
January 1994	Shushkevich is dismissed as Speaker of the parliament.
February 1994	A new Constitution is established in Belarus.
12 April 1994	Russia and Belarus announce a monetary union (abandoned by the Russian side later in the year).
23 June and 10 July 1994	Presidential elections result in victory for Alyaksandr Lukashenka.
January 1995	Belarus joins the NATO Partnership for Peace Program.
January 1995	Russia and Belarus form a customs union.
21 February 1995	Russia and Belarus sign a Treaty of Friendship and Cooperation.
14 May 1995	Parliamentary elections and a national referendum, which votes to change the state symbols and national flag, and supports the elevation of Russian as a state language.
2 April 1996	Belarus and Russia announce the formation of a Community of Sovereign Republics.
26 April 1996	Up to 80,000 participate in Chernobyl march in Minsk and clashes with militia result. Over 200 people arrested.
November 1996	Last of the nuclear weapons are removed from the territory of Belarus.
24 November 1996	Referendum increases powers of the president and divides parliament into two houses: the House of Representatives and the Council of the Republic. A new Constitution is approved for Belarus.
March–August 1997	Repression against the press and nongovernmental organizations.
2 April 1997	Belarus and Russia sign an Act of Union (ratified by the parliaments of both countries in June 1997).

PREFACE

This book forms part of the author's continuing research on Belarus. Its goal is to examine the contemporary situation in Belarus: in politics, society, and the economy, with the intention of providing a useful guide for scholars, university and college students, and for those doing business in or visiting Belarus. It is based on numerous visits to the republic, and extensive library work, interviews, and travel therein. Over the past five years I have travelled widely in the country, though I have generally been based in Minsk. The premise behind the research is (in part) the view that Belarus remains relatively neglected among Western scholars. According to a recent survey of applications for IREX grants for studies on the newly independent republics from the United States, only four were for topics on Belarus, two of which were funded. The author has attended conferences over the past year in Minsk, New York, Boston, and other centers and once again the number of scholars working actively in this academic area—particularly if one excluded those from the Belarusian diaspora—remains small. Belarus is often regarded as a less attractive research site than those in Russia or Ukraine. A repressive political system and difficult living conditions perhaps preclude the arrival of a flock of scholars, descending on the archives like vultures on carrion.

This book is divided into six chapters. Chapter 1 provides a brief history of Belarusian lands from earliest times to the Gorbachev period. Chapter 2 examines the economy over the decade 1986–1996. Chapter 3 looks at the period of perestroyka which, in the Belarusian case, extended beyond the Gorbachev years and the dissolution of the Soviet Union to 1993 (mainly because the most dramatic reversal of this policy occurred not in 1992, but with the election of Alyaksandr Lukashenka as president of Belarus in 1994). Chapters 4 and 5 provide a detailed picture of the tumultuous political changes under Lukashenka, with concentration on domestic issues. The final chapter focuses on Belarusian relations with Russia, including the recent Act of Union.

If there is an underlying theme to this work, it is the fundamental question whether Belarus can survive as an independent state. Has it relinquished its independence already? If it survives, what form will this survival take? The question is not limited to the political maneuvers of the present regime; it also takes into account what has been termed a "demographic catastrophe," the decline of the population in the recent period. I should perhaps state at the outset that I maintain some faith in the survival of a Belarusian state into the next century. It is argued that even under a harsh ruler such as Lukashenka,

Belarusian culture still survives. Also, this book adheres to the view that many of the changes introduced by Lukashenka exist more in theory than in reality, particularly the formation of the Community with Russia in April 1996 and the Act of Union of 1997. There are many basic differences between the two countries so that although they have indubitably drawn closer under the current Belarusian leadership, they are far from joined. Discussion of the various facets of the Union in the future is likely to pull them further apart rather than draw them together.

The book nonetheless may make grim reading. Belarusians have been significantly deprived of their human rights over the past year. Most disturbing is the almost total lack of recourse to assistance in the event of arbitrary arrest. Very few Belarusians have kept up with the new laws that are being introduced almost daily. The press has been systematically silenced; television has become the direct mouthpiece of the president; referenda and elections are ruthlessly manipulated; and society resembles a pyramid with the president at the pinnacle. The revised (new) Constitution, introduced after the referendum of November 1996 is a vehicle for the transfer of all power to the presidency. The tentacles of the presidency had begun by mid-1997 to reach into every sphere of life. Telephones were frequently tapped, demonstrators were beaten and thrown in jail. Foreigners also found that there were no exemptions from arrest or harassment. Most surprising, perhaps, was that despite such repression, the president retained his popularity. Were Belarusians seeking a new Stalin? Or did many of them swallow the official propaganda that those arrested were enemies of the state?

Belarus serves as an example and warning to the other post-Soviet states of the dangers of unlimited presidential power. At the same time, it is not unique in adopting a system that gives the president authority over the legislature. The same can be said of the vast majority of what can be termed "Eurasian nations" since 1991. In such cases, the key factor is the personality of the president, and whether the office is held by an authoritarian reformer, such as Boris Yeltsin in Russia, or a potential dictator with nostalgia for the past like Lukashenka. The observer takes some solace from the fact that the latter leader rules a relatively small nation that does not pose a military threat to its neighbors. Instead, he has been obliged to pursue, more or less constantly, a link or union with Russia.

At various international conferences over the past few years, I have heard frequent comments about this union or integration, and they have often included criticism of Russia. Belarus has been swallowed up by its giant neighbor. As this book was being completed, the Belarusian Popular Front held its Fifth Congress in Minsk (20–21 June 1997), and its leader Zyanon

Paznyak once again focused on "Russian imperialism" and demanded a campaign oriented toward NATO and against Russia. This author would offer a somewhat different interpretation of the events described in this book. While Belarus can, logically, adopt policies that direct the country more toward Europe than Eurasia—which evidently is what Paznyak was requesting—it cannot avoid close association with Russia. One can chastize the extent of Russification or the domination of the Russian language in Belarus, but one cannot deny their existence or eradicate them, in Lukashenka style, by a presidential decree. Paznyak may be ahead of his time.

Further, Russia is rather like the curate's egg, i.e., not everything about it is bad and it provides a variety of influences. On the one hand, it may seem, given past history, like a predator, wishing to link up with and annex its former partners in the USSR. On the other hand, it is partly thanks to Russia that reforms have taken place at all in Belarus. The Russian media has exposed the brutality of some of the actions of the Belarusian militia and presidential guard in 1995–1997. Newspapers, such as *Izvestiya*, constituted a virtual beacon of light in the new period of a censored press. How else are Belarusians to acquire dispassionate views of domestic and international events without the Russian media? Moreover, as noted, Boris Yeltsin has committed his government to the reform process, a factor that Lukashenka cannot ignore. The Belarusian government has few other friends at present.

The solution to Belarusian dilemmas—this book incidentally does not in general offer answers to the many problems facing Belarus, since it is hardly the function of academics to offer advice to politicians—is far more likely to come from the East than the West. And, as we have argued in this book, integration and union remain more on paper than in reality. The process faces severe limitations. The office of the Russian president rarely agrees (and often ignores) the demands or decisions of the Russian Duma. So also, is the new parliamentary congress likely to find that its legislation is no more than advice to the respective governments, to deal with as they wish. Integration can also mean different things to each side. It is far more important for Belarus to maintain its links with Russian reformers and democrats. Economically, the country is unlikely to extricate itself from the Russian orbit. Russia, on the other hand, is hardly seeking an economic millstone around its neck.

The first priority of the researcher, surely, is to enhance public knowledge about the situation in Belarus, a country that only rarely (though more often under Lukashenka than hitherto) makes international headlines. This author has tried to expand his contacts in that country as widely as possible, though invariably he has spent more time with democrats and reformers than with, for example, members of the government, or Communist deputies in the old or new parliaments. I accept criticism for such omissions though my reasoning was that one could learn little new from these sources. Similarly, the views of the presidential administration were available from the pages of newspapers like *Sovetskaya Belorussiya* and *Narodnaya hazeta*, or could be heard nightly on national television. On some occasions it was like suffering from *déjà vu*, as the media so faithfully reflected the views of the government, just as in the Soviet period.

I would like to express special thanks to a number of people who have made my task easier. In Belarus, they include the following: Lyuba Pervushina, Henadz Hrushavy (Gennadiy Grushevoy), Stanislau Shushkevich, Dmitry Kozikis, Serhy Lapteu, Uladzimir Hlod, Yelena Gapova, Natalya Masherauvaya, Adam Maldzis, Alyaksandr Shimko, and Yulia Shimko; in North America: Joe Arciuch, Jan Zaprudnik, David F. Duke, Victoria Plewak, and Paul Goble. A special thanks goes to Paul Fusco of the Magnum group (New York) for providing the cover photograph. A small section in Chapter 2 contains material extracted from an article published in the journal *Post-Soviet Affairs* (Fall 1993), and is reprinted with the kind permission of the publisher, Victor H. Winston.

The book forms part of a major study that is being funded through a major grant from the Social Sciences and Humanities Research Council of Canada. I have also received financial assistance through the Humanities and Fine Arts Council and the Support for the Advancement of Scholarship (Faculty of Arts) funds at the University of Alberta. Several people have provided inspiration, particularly at times when it was difficult to drag oneself back to Minsk yet again to find certain items of information: Piali Das Gupta, Adi Roche, Tim McRory, Susan Smith, Andrew Gow, Rich Connors, and not least, my own graduate students, past and present.

Finally, my family, as always, provided support at all times, and it is to them that I owe the greatest debt: my wife Lan, and sons Carlton and Keelan.

Map of Belarus

Chapter 1

HISTORY OF BELARUS TO 1985

FROM EARLIEST TIMES TO 1917

The early history of Belarus is steeped in controversy. Belarusian scholars rightly note that the country has a history dating back to ancient times, but there is today no consensus on the origins of the Belarusian state. The three tribes from which the Belarusians are believed to have derived were the Krivichi, Dregovichi, and Radimichi, who lived first on the Dvina River and later in the vicinity of the Pripyat and Sozh rivers. The medieval period of Belarusian history dates from the rule of Prince Rahvalod over the Polatsk principality in 980. In the late 10th century, Polatsk was annexed by Vladimir, the ruler of Kievan Rus', who killed the Polatsk prince and married his daughter, Rahneda. At least three principalities existed on what is today ethnically Belarusian territory: that of Smolensk; Polatsk-Vitsebsk; and Turau-Pinsk. Belarusian territory was left relatively unscathed by the Mongol invasions which destroyed Kievan Rus' and the city of Kiev (Kyiv) itself in 1240.

When the Rahvalod dynasty ended in the 14th century, Belarusian territory became part of the Grand Duchy of Lithuania with the capital at Vilna (Vilnius), a state in which Slavs heavily outnumbered the Lithuanians, retained privileges, and in which state business was conducted in the Belarusian language. By the 16th century a distinctive culture had begun to emerge, symbolized by the translation of the Bible into the Belarusian language by Frantsishak Skaryna in 1517. In 1569, however, the Grand Duchy formed a political union with Poland at the Union of Lublin forming the Rzecz Pospolita, and the sovereign of Poland was also the Grand Duke of the Lithuanian kingdom. In this period, Belarusians faced pressure from the Poles to convert from Orthodoxy to Roman Catholicism. The union lasted until the late 18th century, by which time the lands of Belarus had fallen under the control of the Russian Empire as a result of the partitions of Poland that took place in 1772, 1793, and 1795.

The Russian Empire period has been widely perceived as one of repression of cultural and political initiatives on Belarusian territory. In 1839, the Uniate (Greek Catholic) Church in the Polatsk region was dissolved and the former Statute of the Duchy of Lithuania dating to 1588 was prohibited. In 1863 a young Belarusian Kastus Kalinouski played a prominent role in the widespread Polish uprising against Russia, and was publicly executed after his capture in March 1864. Belarusian culture made great strides in the 19th century and it was during this period that the concept of a Belarusian nation first truly emerged. The vast majority of ethnic Belarusians were villagers at the turn of the century. Though industrial development had progressed rapidly in the late 19th century, Belarus lagged behind most territories of the Russian Empire in this respect. The major Belarusian centers, such as Vilna, Minsk, Homel and Mahileu, contained Jewish majorities, with Poles and Russians as the largest minorities in urban area.

THE REVOLUTION PERIOD

In 1905, Belarusians were permitted to publish newspapers and books in their native language, and national activities became more widespread. The most prominent publication was *Nasha Niva* (Our Cornfield), run by the brothers Lutskevich, which became the main Belarusian cultural publication in Vilna until 1915. Overall in the period 1905–1914, a national cultural revival occurred though it was not on a sufficient scale to serve as the basis for state independence from Russia. Though Belarusian territories were to play a part in the revolutionary upheavals of 1905 and 1917, and indeed to witness the declaration of an independent state in the spring of 1918, it is far-fetched to declare that these lands were prepared in any way to form a national state based either on historical precedent or linguistic foundations. Demographically, ethnic Belarusians lived in the countryside rather than the towns.

This situation has been described in detail by the American scholar Steven Guthier, who notes that in 1897, 98% of Belarusians lived in rural areas or in settlements with a population of less than 2,000.[1] An estimated 92% of Belarusians made their livelihood from agriculture, forestry, hunting and fishing. Within the middle and trading classes, Belarusian representation was extremely weak. Belarusians were rarely to be found among the educated stratum. The vast majority were peasants, predominantly illiterate and occupied in small-scale agricultural pursuits that could barely guarantee subsistence. Indeed if one looks at the major cities in Belarusian territories in the 1897 census, the percentage of Yiddish speakers is the most remarkable phenomenon (Vilna, 40%; Minsk, 51.2%; Vitsebsk, 50.8%; Homel, 55.4%; Babruisk, 60.2%, Pinsk, 73.9%).[2]

Clearly Belarusians lacked an urban base from which to launch a claim to statehood. This factor was particularly significant because the Bolshevik Revolution was very much an urban phenomenon. Marxist parties were beginning to develop in Belarus by the late 19th century. Indeed, much has been made of the fact that the Russian Social Democratic Workers' Party held its founding congress in Minsk in 1898, though this was not an event regarded as particularly significant at that time. Alongside the RSDWP was the autonomous Jewish Bund. Together they participated in strike actions in Minsk. In 1902 the Belarusian Revolutionary Party was founded, renamed the Belarusian Socialist Hramada (BSH) in 1903. Thus several marxist groups and cultural-educational organizations were beginning to emerge on Belarusian territory.[3]

The Socialist Hramada had branches in Vilna and St. Petersburg in addition to that in Minsk, and it gained in influence during the February Revolution of 1917, which ended tsarist rule in Belarus. According to one observer, this revolution changed the situation of the Belarusian movement, as the Belarusian peasants began to demand their rights. Simultaneously the Belarusian intelligentsia began to formulate a political program and were particularly active in Minsk. In the summer of 1917 a Belarusian Communist Party emerged from the ranks of the Socialist Hramada, as did a Belarusian Social Democratic Party. Most of the activists of this wing remained in Poland, and it sought autonomous status for Belarus within the confines of a restored Polish state.[4] Much of this activity occurred in a volatile urban environment, but because of the demographic nature of Belarusian territories it did not and could not have involved the majority of Belarusians. There were also significant divisions within the urban Belarusian groups.

Though an independent Belarusian state was declared on 25 March 1918, this state was formed under occupation by the Central Powers and indeed negated by the Treaty of Brest Litovsk signed earlier in the same month between the Central Powers and the Bolshevik regime.[5] This government restored the white, red, white flag and state emblem of the former Grand Duchy of Lithuania (a knight on horseback, a symbol that was to give offense to the first elected president of independent Belarus, Alyaksandr Lukashenka, in 1994). Yet it lacked the means to survive. It was a product of World War I rather than the Russian Revolution and died an inevitable death with the practical application of the results of the Treaty of Brest-Litovsk, the reestablishment of an independent Polish state, and the defeat of the Central Powers in November 1918.

The situation at the end of the First World War was fluid. Two great empires had collapsed—the Russian and the Austro-Hungarian—and however unsatisfactory the peace treaties that were signed in Paris and Riga (at least from the Belarusian perspective), several new nations had emerged in central and eastern Europe (the three Baltic states, Czechoslovakia, and Yugoslavia). In theory Belarus could have been another. Though it was arguably unprepared for statehood, the same could be said of Estonia,

Latvia, and Lithuania. Yet the smaller Baltic states received independence and Belarus did not. Hence, runs one argument, the Western allies must bear the brunt of the blame for their failure to support Belarusian national aspirations and for their polonocentric policies.[6]

All these statements may be true. Certainly the formation of some nations rather than others appears to be arbitrary. Belarus, however, had neither clearly demarcated borders, nor a conception of its past and present national status. What had occurred in March 1918 was not an accident but it was premature. The first steps toward national self-assertion had been taken, but no more than that. Whether or not the BNR could have developed a nation state at this time may always be a moot point. Under the circumstances of 1918, such a state could not have survived for long and its existence was not accepted by the majority of the population living on those territories that today comprise Belarus. We have already noted that the Belarusian elite was a small and persecuted minority, that few Belarusians lived in the cities, and the national past could only be reconstructed through what can best be described as "historical leaps" over centuries of uncertain existence. The progress of Belarusian culture in itself is not an indicator of readiness for or capability of statehood. In 1918, Belarus did not yet have the prerequisites of national statehood. Poland did.

Who then proclaimed independence for Belarus in March 1918? The process was complex. On 19 March, on the initiative of the Belarusian Socialist Hramada, the Council (Rada) of the BNR became a temporary parliament, and all laws issued required the Rada's approval. Most of the Rada members belonged to the BSH party and there were around seventy members altogether. On 24 March, the Rada adopted its third constitutional charter with the participation of the Belarusian Council of Vilna. The Vilna group had initially proclaimed a separate Belarusian-Lithuanian state on 17 December 1917 but now decided to join with the "independentists" of Minsk and separate from Russia. The decision to declare independence followed a BSH proposal for such a move and a noisy and acrimonious 10-hour debate on the night of 24–25 March. Though a majority were in favor, the Jewish Bund was opposed, and many voters decided to abstain, including the United Jewish Socialist Party and the Social Revolutionary Party. Neither the Germans nor the Bolsheviks supported the newly declared state, and indeed the Second Congress of the Soviets of the western province on 14 April denounced the Rada as a counter-revolutionary organ that had been founded by anti-Soviet activists.[7]

Without German support the new state was doomed from the outset. The Vilna Council also continued to exist with its own agenda even after independence had been claimed. The BSH disintegrated, with many of its left-wing adherents deserting the government which by then had associated its interests exclusively with those of the German army: "only under the protection of the German Reich can our country anticipate happiness in the future."[8] The association with German militarism alienated many socialists. It also served to bolster support for the Bolsheviks and weakened the government in the eyes of the public as being incapable of standing alone against its enemies. The present Lukashenka regime in Belarus has even manipulated this association with the Germans to discredit parties such as the BPF which still recognize the validity of the 25 March declaration. However, despite the weaknesses of the campaign for national statehood in 1918, the brief declaration and indeed establishment of independence was to set an important precedent for the promoters of Belarusian culture and self-assertion in the Soviet era.

FORMATION OF THE BSSR

The BSSR was first proclaimed on 1 January 1919 in the city of Smolensk by D. Zhylunovich, Chairman of the "Provisional Worker-Peasant Government" of Belarus. The Manifesto, published two days later in the newspaper *Zvyazda*, declared that all power was in the hands solely of the Soviet workers, peasants, *batraks* (the poorest peasant stratum) and Red Army deputies.[9] The capital of this tiny Soviet republic was the city of Minsk, a city then far from secure from invasion. Five days later, Vilna, the cultural center of historic Belarus, was occupied by the Red Army. On 2–3 February, the First All-Belarusian Congress of workers, peasants, and Red Army deputies was held. It approved the issuance of the first Constitution of the BSSR, established the flag and symbols of the republic, and elected a Central Executive Committee. Progress was threatened, however, by the incursions of the Polish army, which occupied the city of Brest-Litovsk on 19 February. In February–March 1919 therefore, the Soviet authorities decided to join together the Lithuanian and Belarusian republics into an entity termed "Lit-Bel." On 4–6 March in Vilna, the Communist Parties of Lithuania, Western Belarus and Soviet Belarus held a united congress. Subsequently the "Lit-Bel" regime operated in the city of Minsk from the end of April to mid-July 1919.[10]

The Polish–Soviet war put an end to the "Lit-Bel" government and Minsk itself was occupied by the Polish army for almost a year, from August 1919 to July 1920. Once the territories had been reoccupied by the Red Army, a new Soviet republic of Belarus was proclaimed on 31 July. The borders of the BSSR could not be resolved until the formal Soviet–Polish peace treaty at

Riga on 18 March 1921. The treaty, from the Belarusian perspective, was far from favorable, as large areas in the western region, containing a majority of Belarusians in the rural areas, were ceded to the newly independent Polish state. In fact Belarus as a territory was divided into two roughly equal halves. Nicholas P. Vakar points out that Belarusian nationalists were far from dismayed at this development since Belarusians on both sides of the border could campaign in different ways for self-assertion keeping in mind Polish–Soviet hostility and the need of the two larger states to conciliate their Belarusian populations.[11]

The key issue for the Belarusian state initially was its relationship with the Russian Federation. Prior to the Riga Treaty, on 16 January 1921, the two republics had signed an agreement on their economic and military relations, but the ultimate solution to the question awaited investigation by a commission established in the summer of 1922. On 14–18 December, in accordance with Lenin's revisions to the initial conception of Stalin, the BSSR joined the new Union of Soviet Socialist Republics, together with Russia, Ukraine, and the Transcaucasian Republic. The USSR was formally established on 30 December.

The BSSR initially consisted of the city of Minsk and a narrow band of territory around it. Gradually, however, the Soviet authorities expanded the republic, while seeking to promote cultural growth. In November 1923, for example, several districts from the gubernias of Vitsebsk, Homel, and Smolensk were transferred to the new republic. On 3 March 1924, a further sixteen districts that contained a majority of ethnic Belarusians were transferred from the Russian Federation. The addition increased the size of the BSSR from 52,300 to 110,500 square kilometers, while the population almost tripled, rising from 1.5 to 4.2 million people. On 8 August the expanded republic was divided into ten districts, 100 raions and over 1,200 village Soviets. Further consolidation occurred in 1926, when the Rechytsa and Homel districts joined the BSSR, and the area increased to 125,600 square kilometers.[12] One authority suggests that the augmentation of the BSSR was a direct result of campaigning by Belarusian nationalists rather than Soviet benevolence.[13]

BELARUSIANIZATION IN THE 1920s

A second constitution of the BSSR was adopted on 11 April 1927. Together with the growth of the republic, which was well received by the population, the Soviet authorities permitted the cultural development of the BSSR, which continued the movement begun in the 19th century, but which had begun to see real fruition only in the early years of the 20th century. By 11 July 1921, the Belarusian State University was founded. On 30 August 1922, an Institute of Belarusian Culture was opened in Minsk, and on 15 September of this same year the Minsk State and University Library was established (it became known as the Belarusian State Library in May 1926).[14] Generally, historians concur that a systematic policy of "Belarusianization" began in 1924 and lasted until the end of the decade. It included the creation of an All-Belarusian Association of Poets and Writers called *Maladnyak* in 1924, and the honoring of two prominent poets (both of whom were later forced to adhere to the Soviet line), Yanka Kupala (in June 1925) and Yakub Kolas (in October 1926).[15]

The Polish territories might also have served as a source of national rebirth, but the new Polish state was firmly opposed to any form of autonomous Belarusian (or Ukrainian) development. In the 1920s, there is evidence to support assertions that Communism was spreading in Western Belarus as membership continued to rise in the Communist Party of Western Belarus, a branch of the underground Communist Party of Poland; and in the Union of Peasants and Workers. The Polish authorities vacillated initially between a centralized and federalized system of government (the main advocate of the former was Roman Dmowski; of the latter General Josef Pilsudski), but ultimately Polish nationalism prevailed and the government never allowed the promised autonomy for Belarusians or Ukrainians in the eastern provinces.[16]

The situation deteriorated further in the period 1928–1932, when Belarusian villages were forcibly pacified by the Polish military after a series of uprisings and strikes. Though one can detect some efforts at cultural revival in the mid-1930s, the Polish authorities shut Belarusian schools and institutions, employed a policy of enforced Catholicization (in the census of 1931, all Belarusian Catholics were listed as Poles, even if they were not of Polish background and had no knowledge of the Polish language, thus reducing the number of Belarusians in this region from an estimated three million to just under one million people), and imprisoned prominent Belarusian intellectuals and leaders in a notorious concentration camp at Bereza Kartuska, which was founded in the mid-1930s. Soviet sources point out that economically these eastern territories were kept largely under–developed. Most of the major landholders were Poles, and the Belarusian peasantry remained landless or land-hungry, prompting a rise in emigration, and a steady flow of those from the rural areas seeking work in the towns.[17]

Under these circumstances, the BSSR served as the cultural center of Belarusian life. The Soviet authorities emphasized in their propaganda the subjugation of Belarusians in neighboring Poland. On 26 February 1928, for example, Kupala headed a Committee for the Defense of the Western Belarusian Hramada, over 180 activists of which had been put on trial by the Polish authorities for revolutionary activities. The Soviet authorities also extended an open invitation to members of the Belarusian Government-in-Exile in Prague to return to their homeland. A Western scholar notes that the exiles returned in large numbers, including the leader, Vaslau Lastouski, and recognized the BSSR as the legitimate government.[18] One could say that for many of the exiles, the pill of socialism was not difficult to swallow if it was accompanied by a wholesale national and cultural revival, during which time the Russian language virtually disappeared from official business, higher educational institutions, and schools. In this sense the BSSR was the natural offshoot of the Belarusian People's Republic of March 1918 (the BNR).

THE PERIOD OF EARLY STALINISM

The situation was to change abruptly, however, with the adoption of the First Five-Year Plan for the development of industry in May 1929, the beginning of the collectivization of agriculture, and the ramifications in Belarus of Stalin's denunciation of "national deviationism" in the national republics. Indeed the first wave of repressions against "national democracy" in the BSSR dates from 1929–1930, with a campaign against the fictitious League for the Liberation of Belarus (modelled on a similar campaign against another nonexistent group, the Union for the Liberation of Ukraine). None of these events were unique to the BSSR, but it is arguable that the beginning of the repression was particularly severe in the republic, which had made such dramatic progress in national-cultural development to that point. One of the first victims was U.M. Ihnatouski, the first president of the Belarusian Academy of Sciences (founded in October 1928), and director of its Institute of History, who committed suicide on 4 February 1931 during a period of interrogation by the GPU.[19]

The destruction of the national elite during the 1930s has been well documented. It provides an example of one of the most systematic purges of the 20th century leaving alive only a handful of compromised figures in the Belarusian intellectual elite by the end of the decade. Particularly hard-hit were the Belarusian Academy of Sciences, members of the KPB and KPZB, and members of the Union of Peasants and Workers, in addition to writers, poets, artists, musicians, and other cultural figures. One of the more recently documented examples of the repression is the discovery of mass graves in the Kurapaty region just north of Minsk and after considerable procrastination, the Belarusian authorities have acknowledged that the bodies found there were executed by the NKVD between 1937 and 1941 (discussed in Chapter 3). The completeness of the Stalin purge in eradicating cultural development—including a sudden halt to the remarkable progress of the native language—was all the more notable because of the return of exiles in the 1920s. All of the cultural gains of the 1920s were destroyed by the purges. They struck also the party elite. The Communist Party of Belarus lost 40% of its personnel during the purges including almost all its leading figures, and the worst single year was 1937.[20]

COLLECTIVIZATION OF AGRICULTURE

The New Economic Policy introduced into the USSR by Lenin at the 10th Party Congress in 1921 led to the consolidation of a group generally referred to as the "middle peasants." The NEP resulted in the "scissors crisis," whereby prices for scarce industrial goods were much higher than for agricultural products, leading to peasant reluctance to sell grain to the state. This situation was particularly acute in the BSSR because of the failure to develop industry even to the modest levels required in the mid-1920s. In 1925, for example, industrial production in the republic reached only 84% of the pre-war level. At the same time agriculture was far from achieving self-sufficiency and imports of grain from other Soviet republics were required. By 1926, the amount of grain being brought into the republic was twice the level of that brought into the same areas in 1913.[21]

Under these circumstances, Stalin's assault on the "kulak" class took on a particularly insidious form in Belarus because its impact was felt mainly on the middle (serednyak) peasants. In 1927, for example, only 4.7% of peasants households in the BSSR were classified as kulaks, but up to 15% were singled out for "dekulakization" in the early 1930s. In addition, the form of landholding by farmstead (khutor) was targeted by the authorities as contrary to the collective farm mentality being sought in the villages.[22] Many khutors had been established during the Stolypin period (1906–1911) when the Russian premier attempted to consolidate peasant stripholdings into individual farms. They were also part of an agricultural policy developed for the period 1926–1930 by D.F. Pryshchepa, the Chairman of the Belarusian Council of People's Commissars. It was Pryshchepa who was to be the main scapegoat for Stalin's antagonism toward farmsteads and his desire for their replacement by collective farms. By 1929, Pryshchepa and other "Right Opportunists" had been dismissed from the party, at the same time as the historian Ihnatouski was being criticized for the "nationalist deviations" in Belarusian culture.[23]

Collectivization began rapidly once the goals of the First Five-Year Plan had been announced. The All-Union decision of 1 January 1930 warned local party and Soviet organs not to supervise the process "by decree," but conducted the campaign at a frantic pace with a demand for "full collectivization" by 1931. By February 1930, about one-third of Belarusian raions had attained more than 86% collectivization among peasant households. In Mahileu and Mazyr regions over 80% of all households had been collectivized, whereas in Minsk and Babruisk the figure was 41–45%, and in Homel region only 29.1%.[24] The diversity of progress may have resulted from several factors: the concentration of the authorities; local conditions; peasant resistance in certain areas, and so on. The process in the BSSR was similar to that in the rest of the Soviet Union though partially differentiated by its speed. Hundreds of officials arrived in the villages from the towns and in 1930, what had started as "artels" were quickly transformed into peasant communes in which all items of property were subject to collectivization. Some 34,000 "kulak" farms were expropriated at the outset and their owners deported to remote regions of the USSR.

There was a brief respite to the collectivization drive after March 1930, when Stalin published his "Dizzy with Success" speech in *Pravda*, blaming over-zealous officials for the various problems on the new collectives. Predictably, when given a choice, the peasants left the new kolkhozy en masse. Collectivization of the BSSR was partially completed within the first two years, though these early farms were far from stable economically or politically as is evident from the measures taken by the authorities against alleged kulaks after collectivization. In the spring of 1932, notes one scholar, over 1,000 collective farms disintegrated and 55,000 peasant households abandoned them, many simply in order to survive.[25] By January 1933, political sections were created in the Machine Tractor Stations, the organizations created ostensibly to supply machinery to the collectives. The political sections conducted purges of kulaks and other workers for "hostile activities." Collectivization was reportedly completed by 1937, but only after a massive purge of collective farm chairmen, coinciding with the start of the general purge in the country as a whole.

Without question, the collectivization campaign was bewildering to the peasants of the BSSR. Perhaps more than any other single event, it turned the majority of ethnic Belarusians against the Soviet regime and helped to dispel the optimism generated in the 1920s Revival period. The fact that it coincided with an official assault on "national deviationism" has convinced some diaspora scholars that an act of "genocide" was being carried out against the Belarusians.[26] Whether or not such a term can be applied to the

1930s in the BSSR, there is no question that the Soviet authorities, after an initial period that seemed to favor and even sponsor a national and cultural revival, had begun a quest to eradicate all vestiges of Belarusian culture from the life of the republic. Ideological conformity and mass collectivization of agriculture provided the background for a third campaign: that of an industrial upsurge to transform a peasant republic into an industrialized one.

INDUSTRIAL DEVELOPMENT

Prior to the First Five-Year Plan, the BSSR remained relatively undeveloped industrially, even in comparison with other parts of the former Russian Empire. Most ethnic Belarusians were confined to the villages with nine out of every ten people still employed in agriculture.[27] Its impact was first to drive rural residents into the rapidly developing cities, and second to increase substantially the proportion of ethnic Belarusians among the urban community. The initial plan called for an increase of output in heavy industry by 3.3 times in the period 1929–1933. Capital investment was to be raised by 6.5 times over the five years, with over 78% of that investment assigned for the construction of new factories. The BSSR was in a difficult position for the commencement of such an ambitious program in that it lacked the rudimentary infrastructure for the development of heavy industry. It had few raw materials, a lack of specialized cadres, and its existing enterprises were mainly light industries dominated by textiles. The first step therefore was the importation of thousands of qualified workers from other parts of the Soviet Union, particularly from Moscow, Leningrad, and Kharkiv. Many factories had to be reconstructed, others built from scratch. Raw materials such as metal, coal and oil were imported from other regions.[28]

The results of the First Five-Year Plan are impressive, even though they are based on Soviet statistics. In the BSSR it saw the construction of 79 large industrial enterprises, including machine factories, cement works and wood processing combines in Mahileu, Krychau, and Homel respectively. A hydroelectric power station was built at Asipovichy (Mahileu Oblast). A reported 74 large factories were reconstructed on the foundations of earlier enterprises. Gross industrial output rose in the BSSR by 2.7 times, exceeding the level of 1927 by 4.8 times (the plan had specified an increase of 3.7 times).[29] The rise of industrial output in the BSSR was well above the All-Union average, presumably because the starting base was so low. The number of workers per factory more than tripled during the first two years of the plan, while the proportion of workers among the overall population increased from 11.3 to 20% from 1929 to 1932. After the Second Five-Year Plan, 1933–1937, the number of workers exceeded 220,000, over 40% of whom were young people and women.[30]

The process of industrialization, while only beginning in the BSSR—in contrast to some of the more developed regions of the country—was accompanied by a large-scale propaganda campaign which crystallized into the Stakhanov movement in the summer of 1935. It also included "shock work," the brigade movement, the "Izotov movement" (named for another record breaker from the Donbas region) and others. The work methods of Stakhanov's coal mine "Tsentral'naya Irmina" were emulated. Wage rises in this period led to inflation, and workers faced overcrowded apartment buildings and inadequate supplies of food. They worked, as noted, in a politically repressive climate in which failure to meet the work norms and plans could result in the harshest punishments.

One can make some general conclusions about industrial development in the mid to late 1930s. Though the pace appeared frenetic, at the end of the decade Belarus was still predominantly an agricultural republic. What was to become known as Eastern Belarus, because of the incorporation of the western region into Poland during the interwar period, had a workforce that comprised no more than 5.5% of the total population. The emphasis, moreover, was on the construction of large enterprises in heavy industry, many of which were still under construction at the end of the decade.[31] Though many Belarusians had moved into the cities, one can still say that even by the end of the Third Five-Year Plan, the vast majority of Belarusians were village-based. That proportion was to be increased quite dramatically by the incorporation of the territory termed "Western Belarus."

THE INCORPORATION OF WESTERN BELARUS

The reasons for the annexation of Western Belarus in September 1939 have long been debated. Generally, historians are skeptical about the official Soviet version of events, which is that the Red Army decided to take these territories under its protection once the government of Poland had collapsed. Some see the incorporation as a machiavellian act carried out under the auspices of the Molotov-Ribbentrop Non-Aggression Treaty. The Soviet interpretation of the situation of Belarusians under Polish rule has also been one-sided, namely that these areas were left underdeveloped, that the best land was in the hands of Polish officials and landowners, and that throughout the period of Polish rule, the local Belarusians waged an unremitting campaign for their freedom and (according to most accounts) for a reunion with their compatriots on the other side of the border.[32]

As with most Soviet accounts, there is a grain of truth in the analysis that can serve to mislead the observer. In the 1920s, as noted, there was considerable political activity on the left of the political spectrum, and the KPZB was a significant underground force, while the Belarusian Association of Peasants, Belarusian Christian Democracy (after 1936 the Belarusian National Association),[33] and the Belarusian Hramada offered some hope for Belarusians in the legal political spectrum. Polish rule was indubitably harsh, so much so that the Soviet invasion seems to have been genuinely welcomed in the western regions. For a brief period in the 1920s, the BSSR had appeared the authentic repository of the cultural aspirations of nationally conscious Belarusians. Moreover, the true nature of the Stalin regime was concealed from many residents of Western Belarus. Politically disaffected— an estimated 10–11,000 people were imprisoned for participation in the Communist movement in the 1930s[34]—many viewed any form of change as positive. Over 90% of the population was engaged in agriculture, but according to a Soviet source, 85,000 farms were landless, and 180,000 households farmed areas of less than one hectare.[35]

On 17 September the Red Army entered Western Belarus, together with Western Ukraine, dividing the Polish state into two between the German-occupied and Soviet-occupied parts. By 22 September, the army had reached Brest, the westernmost city of what was to become the new BSSR. Belarusian territories were thus united, though the border between them was never opened prior to the outbreak of war. The authorities announced elections to a People's Assembly and those elections took place on 22 October, exactly five weeks after the invasion. Every effort was made to ensure widespread participation in the election and Red Army soldiers were permitted to participate. Over 96% of those eligible to vote took part, and 90.7% supported the selected candidate. 926 deputies were duly elected to attend the assembly, which met in Bialystok on 28 October. Belarusians were heavily favored during this election, particularly over the Poles. Thus 621 deputies were Belarusians, 127 Poles, and 72 Jews, though the proportion of Belarusians in Western Belarus was probably no more than 40%.[36] The assembly debated four questions: state power; the incorporation of Western Belarus into the BSSR; the confiscation of the estates of the landowners; and the nationalization of banks and heavy industry.[37] The key issue, however, was annexation of the territories to the USSR, and the Assembly elected 66 plenipotentiaries to attend the V Session of the Supreme Soviet in Moscow, held from 31 October to 2 November 1939. The latter duly affirmed this ritualistic process, as did the meeting of the Supreme Soviet of the BSSR on 12–14 November.

As a result of the "reunion" of Belarusian territories, the BSSR was increased by 45% in area and 46% in population. The republic thus almost doubled in size. At the same time, the population voting in the elections was unaware that the Soviet authorities had reached an agreement with Lithuania, ceding both the city of Vilna and the Vilna region to that republic, evidently in exchange for the right to establish Soviet military bases there. The concession was not merited on ethnic grounds, as Belarusian writers have pointed out. According to the Polish census of 1931, only 1,400 Lithuanians out of a population of 193,300 lived in the city of Vilna (Vilnius), or 0.7%. In the area as a whole, Belarusians comprised about 50% of the population, and Lithuanians 18%. Moreover, Vilna was of special concern to nationally conscious Belarusians as the city of Belarusian cultural rebirth. Altogether Lithuania received in 1939–1940 9,500 square kilometers of territory with a population of about 534,000. The Soviet regime, and Molotov specifically, declared that it had taken into account that Vilna was the capital of the ancient Grand Duchy of Lithuania.[38]

Initially, the amalgamated BSSR was based on five new oblasts: Baranavichi, Bialystok, Vilna, Brest, and Pinsk; with 101 rayons (districts). The incorporation of the western territories placed Minsk firmly at the center of the reconstituted republic. The area of the republic increased from 125,600 to 223,000 square kilometers, and the population from 5.6 to 10.2 million (taking into account the loss of the city of Vilna and surrounding region). Soviet rule began cautiously, particularly given the absence of party personnel, who had to be transferred piecemeal from the eastern regions over the course of the next twenty-one months. The People's Assembly expropriated 3,325 large farms of more than 50 hectares in size, distributing a reported 1,180,000 hectares of land among the land-hungry peasant households. Much of the confiscated land was retained for the formation of collective and state farms. By the outbreak of war, 1,115 collective farms (6.7% of all households) and 28 state farms had been established on the territory of Western Belarus and reportedly the collectives were larger and more stable than their eastern counterparts at the same stage of collectivization.[39]

There was no attempt, however, to impose mass collectivization and by establishing a small number of collective farms, the authorities could ensure that they received ample supplies and were well organized. Though the border between the two parts of Belarus remained closed, the western regions were once again permitted to develop some aspects of Belarusian culture. Indeed the territories were "Belarusianized." Soviet benevolence, however, was short-lived. By the early spring of 1940, the western regions were subjected to repressions, beginning with the deportation of some 25,000 (principally Polish) state officials.[40] Though not well documented, the Belarusian population appears to have been targeted subsequently by the NKVD, with executions of potential malcontents and alleged opponents of the Soviet regime. Many others were imprisoned. The Stalin regime was fearful of territories that had for so long been subjected to "bourgeois rule." When the Germans invaded in June 1941, many of these prisoners were massacred prior to the hasty retreat of the Soviet authorities.[41]

THE GERMAN INVASION

The BSSR was invaded by the German army on 22 June 1941. About 3.2 million troops crossed the Soviet border at 4am Moscow time, and the BSSR lay in the path of Army Group Center, which was directed ultimately at the city of Moscow. The immediate results for the Soviet side were catastrophic. The Luftwaffe destroyed 1,200 planes, mostly on the ground, of which 738 lay on Belarusian territory. The thrust was rapid and decisive in the western and central regions. Within six days, the capital Minsk had fallen to the enemy, though the other cities fell after more sustained resistance throughout the course of the year. Homel, for example, was captured only on 19 December, and Mazyr on 22 December. Nonetheless, by the end of 1941 all the BSSR territory lay in the hands of the German occupants.

As in September 1939 with the Red Army, many residents of the BSSR welcomed the invasion. Some recalled the German occupation of 1918 and compared it favorably with the rule of Poles and Soviets. In the western regions in particular, there appears to have been an unwillingness to oppose the invader, which contributed to the encirclement of major Soviet armies in the first weeks of the war. In addition, the official Soviet response to the invasion was slow: beginning with disbelief, particularly on the part of Stalin; the creation of a State Defense Committee on 30 June; a directive of the Central Committee of the Communist Party of Belarus, "Concerning the development of partisan warfare in the rear of the enemy," on 1 July; and finally Stalin's address to the nation of 3 July. For Belarusians the call for partisan activity was not immediately transformed into reality. The partisans were at first comprised of small disorganized groups. The central authorities in Moscow were concerned about the development of an autonomous movement in the occupied regions of the BSSR and wanted to subordinate operations to the NKVD.

The German occupants had little use for anti-Soviet actions on the part of the local population during the first two years of the war. Rather, they chose to divide up Belarusian lands into different administrative units, and to use

Belarus as an area of German "lebensraum." Officially Belarus was part of "Ostland" (the eastern lands), together with the Baltic states. White "Russland" consisted only of the central region, including the cities of Minsk, Lida, and Slutsk. Bialystok was appended to East Prussia and Vilna region remained part of Lithuania under German occupation. German military rule was imposed east of the Berezina River. The Germans thus paid little attention to aspirations for independence. In addition, even before the occupation of Belarus was complete, Jews in the major cities (Minsk and Hrodna in particular) were moved into ghettos or into concentration camps being established in the vicinity.[42]

There is general consensus among historians about the harsh results of German rule. The official Soviet figures report that during the period of occupation, Belarus lost 2,219,316 of its population, one of the highest proportions of any area in the war. A total of 209 cities (out of 270) and 9,200 villages had been ruined.[43] Some of the most destructive battles occurred when the Red Army reentered the territory of the BSSR on 26 November 1943 and throughout 1944, hence at least a portion of the destruction must have accrued from conflict and weapons used by both sides. Partisan warfare was centered largely in the territory of the occupied BSSR and by November 1943 there were some 122,600 partisans operating there. As I have noted elsewhere, some 78% of partisans began their operations in 1943.[44] Soviet sources, by contrast, tend to stress their involvement from the very outset of war. By September 1943, a Minsk underground committee of the Communist Party of Belarus was also in operation while on 17 February 1944 the Soviet State Defense Committee created the army of the First Belarusian Front under the command of the Warsaw-born general, K.K. Rokossovsky. Thus by late 1943 and 1944 it can be stated with certainty that the tide of war had turned and that ultimately the Red Army would emerge victorious.

What is less certain is the intention of the German occupation regime in the BSSR. Prior to the invasion, in the summer of 1940, a Belarusian Self-Aid Committee had been established in Berlin, headed by A. Barouski, the former consul of the Belarusian People's Republic of 1918.[45] After the war began, a similar organization was formed in October 1941, led by I. Yermachenka, formerly chairman of the Belarusian Committee in Prague.[46] Another prominent organization was the Belarusian Nationalist Party, founded in June 1940 in Warsaw under the leadership of Jan Stankevich. Belarusians abroad took encouragement from the speech made by Hitler on 21 July 1940, in which he declared that after a German invasion of the Soviet Union, three separate republics would be formed: Belarus; Ukraine; and a Baltic federation.[47] In brief, a number of Belarusian exiles hoped to take advantage of the coming German invasion to push for Belarusian interests in the occupied territory and perhaps even to attain an independent state.

Thus when the German civilian administration was established in Minsk under Wilhelm Kube, there appeared to be some scope for a revival of Belarusian life in the occupied BSSR. Kube made elementary education compulsory for all children (except Jews) aged 7–14, prohibited the use of Russian textbooks, and allowed the Belarusianization of what might be termed the lower administration led by a nationalist leader, Radislau Astrouski. He also permitted the establishment of a Belarusian Autocephalous Orthodox Church. The appeal of the occupation regime was limited both by excesses during the war and by the growing encroachment of the partisans and pro-Soviet forces. In the summer of 1943 and early 1944 a Belarusian Central Council was formed and given authority to conscript 100,000 troops to the Belarusian Land Defense in a belated attempt to change the course of the war. Also in December 1943, Astrouski became president of the Belarusian National Rada, which called an All-Belarusian Congress in Minsk on 27 June 1944, less than one week before the city was overrun by the Soviet army.[48]

The above events are outlined only to indicate the complexity of the situation in the occupied BSSR. Soviet (and even post-Soviet) accounts of the Great Patriotic War on Belarusian territory are largely confined to details of the repressive nature of the regime, the heroism of the partisans, and the ultimate triumph of the Soviet army, which was obliged to take on the mantle of saving the civilized world from German National Socialism. The war, however, brought forth a flood not only of patriotism, but also of Belarusian aspirations for a new revival (especially among young people), and particularly in the pivotal year 1943 when the retreating German army brought in its wake a flood of refugees of all hues seeking to escape from Soviet territory.

WITHDRAWN

THE EARLY POSTWAR YEARS (1945–1965)

The pro-Soviet partisans were the only Belarusian group to emerge from the war intact and with their prestige at the highest level. Because of the brutal and destructive nature of the German-Soviet conflict and the survival of the Soviet state and system against seemingly insuperable odds, the Soviet regime began to create propagandistic myths centered on the war. It became one of the prime justifications for Soviet rule, supplanting even the October Revolution as the pivotal event of Soviet history. For many Soviet residents—in Central Asia, Siberia, the Far East, for example—such propaganda may have seemed far-fetched. For Belarusians, however, the differences

SPRING CREEK CAMPUS

between the official Soviet version of events and the reality was, at the very least, blurred. Liberation had come from the east. The conqueror was Stalin, ably assisted by K.K. Rokossovsky, K.A. Vershinin, G.K. Zhukov, T.T. Khryukin, and other outstanding military leaders, and the local partisans were the definitive and lasting symbols of that resistance.

The impact of the war on the population has been discussed above. In terms of costs, it has been estimated that the damage amounted to R75 billion (in 1941 prices) or the equivalent of 35 annual budgets similar to that of 1940.[49] The border was readjusted once again as the Curzon Line was established by the Allied powers as the legitimate eastern border of Poland. Seventeen raions of the Bialystok region and three raions of the Brest Oblast were transferred to Poland. Between 1944 and 1948 a population exchange took place between the two states: about 274,200 Poles moved out of the BSSR into Poland, and a much smaller number of Belarusians—about 37,000— moved from Poland into the BSSR.[50] The BSSR was permitted a seat at the United Nations (along with Ukraine), ostensibly because of the sacrifices suffered during the German occupation. The decision was ratified by the Supreme Soviet of the BSSR on 30 August 1945. Internally, the BSSR was given its own Commissariat as early as March 1944 (and two years later it was retitled Ministry) of Foreign Affairs.[51]

After the war, further repressions ensued, partly as a result of persistent guerrilla activities conducted against the renewal of Soviet rule in the western regions of Belarus in the late 1940s. These activities were particularly acute during the collectivization of farms in Western Belarus, which was modelled on the process carried out in the eastern regions in the 1930s. Collectivization was accompanied by the establishment of Machine-Tractor Stations (there were seventy-eight by the end of 1949), and political sections of the MTS in early 1950 to root out hostile elements within the new collective farms. Progress was noticeably slow and only at the end of 1952 was the process completed, when 540,300 peasant households were collectivized, 95% of the total number. In this same year, 4,431 "kulak" families were deported from the BSSR to Kazakhstan, Yakutsk, Kirghizia, and other regions.[52]

The party leadership was thoroughly purged in the period 1947–1950, and the leadership of the republic was in the hands of a Ukrainian (P. Ponomarenko) and Russians (N. Gusarov, N. Patolichev). In the period of the "Zhdanovshchina," any remaining manifestations of Belarusian nationalism or Belarusian culture were eliminated. As one source has noted, the intellectual elite of the republic was destroyed,[53] a repression that evoked memories of the purges of the 1930s. In fact any token manifestation of a separate Belarusian identity was branded as "bourgeois nationalism" and equated with collaborationism during the war. As the intellectual leadership was removed, it was replaced by Stalinist appointees. Yet the partisan leaders also remained and, once the repressions ended with the death of Stalin in 1953 and particularly after the 20th All-Union Party Congress of 1956, were in position to take over the leadership of the republic.

By the time of the Khrushchev "thaw" the pro-Soviet partisan leaders, led by K.T. Mazurau and P.M. Masherau, dominated Belarusian party politics. Since the 1920s there had been little scope for the development of the Belarusian language and culture. In this respect Belarus was no different from most other Soviet republics. Its uniqueness lay in the stability of its Communist authority in the postwar era, the singular ability of Belarusian leaders to pursue republican interests exclusively through the Soviet party and government structure. Few Soviet republics could equate national and Soviet interests so closely. Belarusians may have had little choice since their intellectual leadership was either in exile or purged.

The process did not begin with this individual, but perhaps its most power-ful manifestation was that which occurred under his administration, namely, Kiryl T. Mazurau, the First Party Secretary of the Belorussian SSR from 1956 to 1965 and subsequently a full member of the CC CPSU Politburo. Mazurau, the first Belarusian to head the party apparatus, used the Belarusian language in official speeches. He was also the leader of a group called the Partisans, made up of those who had made a name for themselves resisting the German occupation regime on Belarusian territory during the Second World War. That the Soviet authorities were prepared to allow a Belarusian ethnic group to take over the mantle of the republic reflects both a certain lib-eralization in Moscow and simultaneously their confidence in the loyalty of such statesmen to the system they had defended so rigorously during the war years. Yet there were always limits to such loyalty and it came with a price, namely the promotion of republican concerns sometimes to the exclusion of overriding Soviet state interests. This became even more evident under the leadership of Mazurau's protege and successor in Belarus, Pyotr Masherau.

THE MASHERAU YEARS, 1965–1980

Before turning to Masherau specifically, a word of explanation is in order. It can be argued that the Belarusian partisans were among the most fanatically loyal to the Soviet system.[54] They could be described as ideological Commun-ists; those who believed in the infallibility of the Soviet structure. At the same time there was, in their view, no apparent contradiction between accepting the current Moscow-dominated apparatus and working within it to secure advancement for their native republic. Belarus was essentially a "have not" republic in terms of developed and even potential natural resources. It could nonetheless be developed industrially and become a prime center of manufacturing machinery and other industries. Because it began as an economically "backward" republic, at least in terms of developed industry, its progress was all the more remarkable once it did embark on the industrialization route. The Communist leaders were personally linked to such "successes" by the public. Belarusians were markedly outspoken in this regard.

If one examines Soviet statistics on industrial progress purely for comparison among the various union republics, then the success of Belarus is immediately evident. In terms of gross industrial output in the period 1970–80, the All-Union increase (1970=100) was reportedly 178; that in the BSSR 232. In terms of labor productivity, the respective figures are 156 for the USSR as a whole and 179 for the BSSR. In both cases the Belarusian total outstripped those of all the other republics, sometimes by a considerable margin.[55] While Soviet statistics are notoriously unreliable as an indicator of actual economic conditions, there is little reason to doubt the republican comparisons. The progress of Belarus was unprecedented and the public would have been made aware of the fact by the party leadership and party and government press. In his speech to the 25th Congress of the All-Union Communist Party, Masherau could not resist lauding the performance of his republic in industry, which had well exceeded plan requirements. National income, he reported, had risen by 47% over the plan period; gross output had increased by 64% rather than the 53–56% anticipated; while the plan itself had been completed five months ahead of time.[56]

The period of Masherau remains among the most notable for the development and assertiveness of Belarus within the Soviet system. Succeeding Mazurau as the party leader in 1965, Masherau was by Soviet standards a charismatic figure, popular among Belarusians and supervising a period of notable industrial growth and well-being. As the leader of the Partisans, he was highly patriotic, hawkish on foreign policy (he was, for example, a rigid opponent of detente which he regarded as a compromise with the enemy) and in many respects a model and ideological Communist.[57] Thus Masherau was a far from typical Brezhnev apparatchik, though he only took the highest office in the first years of the Brezhnev-Kosygin administration. He remained dedicated to Belarusian interests to the extent that some of his colleagues in Moscow regarded him as a potentially dangerous nationalist. This was symbolized by his appearing in public in national costume and speaking the native language at some official functions.[58]

Masherau has been compared to the Ukrainian party leader, Petro Shelest, both in outlook and politics.[59] Whereas Shelest was removed in 1972, however, and replaced by a Russophile hardliner in Volodymyr Shcherbytsky, Masherau remained at his post, protected by the patronage of Mazurau, by now a member of the CC CPSU Politburo in Moscow. Masherau never advanced beyond the status of a Candidate Member of the Politburo. One reason for his slow progress may have been that in Mazurau, this small republic already had a senior Politburo member; two may have seemed excessive. Equally plausible is the theory that Masherau was never fully accepted by the Brezhnev leadership as a man willing to follow central *diktat*. As the noted American political scientist Amy Knight has shown, Mazurau was also backed by Kosygin rather than Brezhnev, a factor that was to lead to his disgrace in a Politburo often cited for its stability and lack of change. In reality, the Brezhnev-Kosygin alliance was not to last and with Kosygin's decline his proteges, including Mazurau, also fell from grace.[60] By 1977, Mazurau was no longer appearing at official functions.[61]

The period 1977–1980 therefore was an uncomfortable one for Masherau in Minsk, as one of his biographers attests. Uladzimir Yakutou notes that among his family and friends, the Belarusian leader was reserved and skeptical about the situation in the leadership of the country and party, often remarking that the problems were impossible to overcome. Even in the Politburo itself he regularly voiced criticism, particularly about the actions of "certain secretaries of the CC CPSU." His daughter Yelena reportedly declared that "around him was created a vacuum."[62] The period coincided with two important events in Moscow: Brezhnev's illness as a result of strokes in 1975 and 1977; and the creation of a personality cult around the ailing Soviet leader. By 1977, Brezhnev was the Commander in Chief of the armed forces and a Marshal of the Soviet Union, and he had added the title of President to his General Secretaryship. It became a ritual for Soviet party and government leaders to praise Brezhnev in every public speech. Thus even the mildest form of dissent from official policy was easily discernible. For the former partisan Masherau, such manifestations of corruption at the highest level must have been a bitter pill to swallow.

Masherau, however, was not a dissident at the outset. Indeed his speeches at the 25th Party Congress in 1976 are notable for their sycophantic and exaggerated obsequiousness toward Brezhnev.[63] He appears to have been as prepared as any other leader to follow ritual as long as the leadership in Moscow pursued a firm foreign policy and did not appear to divert from the principles of Marxism-Leninism. After the removal of Mazurau from the CC CPSU Politburo and the emergence of a Brezhnev cult, the leadership of the

Partisans was systematically undermined in Belarus, however. Before long, the tone of Masherau's speeches had changed markedly. It had become evident that the Belarusian party elite had distanced itself from the Moscow leadership and as such was targeted for removal.

According to one account, the enmity originated in the early 1970s, following Brezhnev's first visit to the republic and his realization that Masherau was acting more independently than most republican party leaders. Masherau was also known to be on bad terms with the key figure of Mikhail Suslov, often described as the power in the background during the Brezhnev administration.[64] Other opponents of the policies being propagated in the republic were reportedly premier N.V. Podgorny, and Brezhnev protege and future CC CPSU General Secretary, Konstantin Chernenko. One example of the deteriorating relations between Moscow and Minsk was the fact that although Minsk was awarded in 1970, the status of Hero City for its exploits in the Second World War a further four years passed before the order was actually signed by Brezhnev.[65] In August 1980, when Masherau made a speech in Alma-Ata at the commemoration of the 60th anniversary of the formation of the Kazakh SSR, Brezhnev was reportedly so disgusted with its contents that he averted his face in "undisguised irritation."[66]

By 1980, Masherau had been isolated by the Brezhnevite clique. Without his patron, Mazurau, his position had become untenable. Among Belarusians, however, his prestige evidently reached its peak at this same time. Masherau stood out as a beacon of honesty and moral rectitude during a period when corruption elsewhere was widespread and even the norm among the bureaucratic elite. In the fall of 1980 Masherau published a book entitled *Sovetskaya Belorussiya*, which highlighted the problems of a leadership that did not listen to the working masses and suffered from arrogance and conceit. The book included a one-sided account of the economic successes of the BSSR, only belatedly offering "thanks to the first among equals, the great Russian people."[67] He then focused on the critical need for youth education and the development of the individual, particularly under the conditions of a "sharply intensifying ideological struggle in the international arena."[68] Was Masherau criticizing his bosses in Moscow? It seems likely. Moreover, as Amy Knight has noted,[69] the book contained hardly a word of praise for Brezhnev. Under the circumstances of the personality cult such an omission could only have been considered a veiled insult to the Soviet leadership.

The Brezhnev years, which coincided roughly with the period of office of Masherau, were also notable for the Russification of the BSSR. Arguably the process began in the 1930s and was stepped up after the war. Between 1959 and 1970, both years in which a national census was undertaken, the Russian language made gains on Belarusian in almost every facet of life, and particularly in the major cities. A Western scholar has thus pointed out that whereas Belarusian speakers comprised a majority in the capital in 1950, by 1970, 54.5% of Minsk residents cited Russian as their native language, and that the biggest rise among Russian speakers was among ethnic Belarusians themselves.[70] A similar decline occurred in the area of publishing. In 1970, for example, 37.3% of all books in circulation were in Belarusian, and 36.5% of all newspapers. A decade later the respective figures were 21.4% and 34.0%.[71] By 1979, even the Minister of Education, Mikhail Minkevich, was complaining that all educational training in the BSSR was being conducted in the Russian language.[72]

CONCLUSION

Contemporary Belarusians tend to look to the Soviet past with nostalgia. The republic experienced a period of remarkable urban growth in the 1960s and 1970s to match the economic progress. A republic that was essentially rural prior to the war experienced one of the most rapid periods of urbanization in history. Moreover, as a result of the various partitions and additions to the existing state Minsk—the very center and fulchrum of party operations—became the dominant center. More than 25% of the urban population and over one-sixth of the total population of Belarus resided in Minsk. The city was the cultural center, the heart of the educational system and of virtually all publishing.[73] It also remained the heart of the official media. In the Soviet period, the Communist Party apparatus in Minsk was among the most powerful and deeply entrenched in the USSR.

Under these circumstances, the path for the pro-democracy forces was always going to be a difficult one. The BSSR had developed as a strongly Communist republic in which many of the leading figures had gained their authority through the party and state structure. There had been no significant movement for change, and the BSSR had initially satisfied urges for a unified state, albeit in a Soviet form. It had reunited ethnic Belarusian territories. Yet at the same time it had become heavily Russified and Sovietized. The impetus for change in 1985, as in 1919, came from outside Belarusian territories.

1 Steven L. Guthier, "The Belorussians: National Identification and Assimilation, 1897–1970. Part 1, 1897–1939," *Soviet Studies*, Vol. XXIX, No. 1 (January 1977): 37–61.
2 Ibid., p. 45.
3 V.M. Ihnatouski, *Karotki narys histor'ii Belarusi* (Minsk: Belarus, 1992), pp. 172–173.
4 Jerzy Tomaszewski, *Rzeczpospolita Wielu Narodów* (Warsaw, 1985), pp. 109, 121.

5   See, for example, Nicholas P. Vakar, *Belorussia: The Making of a Nation: A Case Study* (Cambridge, Mass.: Harvard University Press, 1956), p. 103.

6   The arguments are summarized in ibid., p. 106.

7   R. Platonov, N. Stashkevich, "Ternistyi put' k svobode," *Neman*, No. 10 (1992): 139–141.

8   Cited in Vakar, *Belorussia: The Making of a Nation*, p. 105.

9   "Iz Manifesta Vremmenogo Raboche-Krest'yanskogo Sovetskogo pravitelstva Belorussii," 1 January 1919, cited in *Kommunist Belorussii*, No. 12 (December 1978): 70.

10   Academy of Sciences of Belarus, Institute of History, *Narysy histor'ii Belarusi*, part 2, ed. M.P. Kastsyuk (Minsk: "Belarus'," 1995), p. 69. [Hereafter *Narysys histor'ii Belarusi*.]

11   Vakar, *Belorussia: The Making of a Nation*, p. 118.

12   Institute of Party History, CC CPB. *V edinoy sem'e bratskikh narodov* (Minsk: Belarus', 1971), p. 11.

13   J. Mienski, "The Establishment of the Belorussian SSR," *Belorussian Review*, No. 1 (1955): 31.

14   Institute of Art, Ethnography, and Folklore, Academy of Sciences, BSSR, *Cultural Policy in the Byelorussian Soviet Socialist Republic* (Paris, 1979), p. 21.

15   For a detailed account of Belarusianization in the 1920s, see *Narysy histor'ii Belarusi*, pp. 127–143.

16   Vakar, *Belorussia: The Making of a Nation*, p. 120.

17   See, for example, I.S. Kravchenko, *Sotsialisticheskoe stroitel'stvo v zapadnykh oblastyakh BSSR (materialy k sessii)* (Tallinn, 1954), p. 2.

18   Vakar, *Belorussia: The Making of a Nation*, p. 144.

19   See, for example, Jan Zaprudnik, *Belarus: At A Crossroads in History* (Boulder, CO: The Westview Press, 1993), p. 87.

20   See, for example, Rostislav Platonov, "Epidemiya zla," *Belaruskaya dumka*, No. 1 (1993): 52–56; and No. 2 (1993): 64–68.

21   V.I. Halubovich, ed., *Ekanamichnaya historyya Belarusi* (Minsk: NKF "Ekaperpesktyva", 1996), p. 239.

22   On the khutors, see, for example Diana Eibert, "Iz istorii khutorov v Sovetskoy Belorussii (1923–1941)," in Ministry of Education, *Historyya Belarusi* (1994): 168–176.

23   N.V. Kuznetsov, "Kollektivizatsiya: trudnye puti," In Platonov, R.P., ed. *Stranitsy istorii Kompartii Belorussii: suzhdeniya, argumenty, fakty* (Minsk: Universitetskoe, 1990), pp. 129–130.

24   *Narysy histor''ii Belarusi*, p. 165.

25   Kuznetsov, "Kollektivizatsiya: trudnye puti," p. 134.

26   See, for example, Symon Kabysh, "Genocide of the Byelorussians," in Vitaut Kipel and Zora Kipel, eds., *Byelorussian Statehood: Reader and Bibliography* (New York: Byelorussian Institute of Arts and Sciences), pp. 229–243; Zaprudnik, *Belarus: At A Crossroads in History*, p. 86, uses the same term as a subheading for the description of the Purges in Belarus.

27   Halubovich, *Ekanamichnaya historyya Belarusi*, p. 416; Guthier, "The Belorussians," Part 1, p.54.

28   *Istoriya Belorusskoy SSR*, ed. I.M. Ignatenko et al (Minsk: Nauka i tekhnika, 1977), pp. 297–298. [Hereafter *Istoriya Belorusskoy SSR.*]

29   *Narysy histor'ii Belarusi*, p. 157.

30   *Istoriya Belorusskoy SSR*, pp. 299–301.

31   S.N. Malinin and K.I. Shabun, *Ekonomicheskaya istoriya BSSR* (Minsk: Vysheyshaya shkola, 1969), pp. 210–211.

32   See, for example, V. Minaev, *Zapadnaya Belorussiya i Zapadnaya Ukraina pod gnetom panskoy Pol'shi* (Moscow: Voenizdat, 1939).

33   Mikolaj Iwanow, "The Byelorussians of Eastern Poland under Soviet Occupation," in Keith Sword, ed., *The Soviet Takeover of the Polish Eastern Provinces, 1939–41* (London: The Macmillan Press, 1991), p. 256.

34   Boris Kleyn, "Zapadnaya Belorussiya: Ot illuziy k realnosti," *Neman*, No. 9 (1989): 128.

35   Kravchenko, *Sotsialisticheskoe stroitel'stvo*, p. 2.

36   *Narysy histor'ii Belarusi*, p. 257.

37   IPH (1971), p. 53.

38   See, for example, Aleksandr Shagun, "Kak perekraivalis' granitsy Belorussii," *Sem' dney*, No. 18 (1990): 6.

39   V.N. Mikhnyuk, "Istoriografiya pervykh sotsialisticheskikh preobrazovaniy v sel'skom khozyaystva zapadnykh oblastey Belorussii," in *Tridtsat' let po sotsialisticheskomu puti. 2.*

Sotsial'no-ekonomicheskie itogu kollektivizatsii (Vilnius, 1979), pp. 189–190; A. Sorokin, "Razgrom: Kak bol'sheviki 'preobrazovali' belorusskuyu derevnyu," *Chalavek i ekanomika*, No. 12 (1994): 35.

40 Mikhnyuk, "Istoriografiya pervykh sotsialisticheskikh preobrazovaniy," p. 190.

41 See, for example, Vakar, *Belorussia: The Making of a Nation*, p. 171.

42 Zaprudnik, *Belarus: At A Crossroads in History*, pp. 95–96.

43 *Narysy histor'ii Belarusi*, p. 322–323, provides a detailed breakdown of war casualties by region.

44 David R. Marples, *Belarus: From Soviet Rule to Nuclear Catastrophe* (Basingstoke,UK: The Macmillan Press, 1996), p. 19. Zaprudnik, *Belarus: At A Crossroads in History*, p. 99, notes that by May 1943 75,000 Soviet "guerrillas" were operating in occupied Belarus, thus one could qualify further the above statement and state that the mass partisan movement dates from the second half of 1943.

45 Jerzy Turonek, *Bialorus pod okupacja niemiecka* (Warsaw: Ksiazka i Wiedza, 1993), p. 40.

46 Aleksey Litvin, "Belorusskaya kraevaya oborona: K voprosu o sozdanii belorusskogo natsional'nogo voyska v gody mirovoy voiny," *Neman* (April 1994): 176.

47 Turonek, *Bialorus pod okupacja niemiecka*, p. 46.

48 Litvin, "Belorusskaya kraevaya oborna,: pp. 184–185.

49 *Istoriya Belorusskoy SSR*, p. 434.

50 G.I. Kasperovich, *Migratsiya naseleniya v goroda i etnicheskie protsessy* (Minsk, 1985), p. 40.

51 A. G. Kokharnovsky, ed., *Istoriya Belarusi* (Minsk: IP "Ekoperspektiva", 1997), p. 270.

52 *Narysy histor'ii Belarusi*, p. 334.

53 Vakar, *Belorussia: The Making of a Nation* , p. 218.

54 I have omitted one major question from this chapter. The partisan movement initially was divided between those who wished to operate according to local initiatives, and those who were brought under centralized NKVD control, as desired by Stalin's close associate, Lavrentiy Beria. The latter group ultimately triumphed though this fact hardly belittles the sacrifices made by the partisans on Belarusian territory. On the differences between the partisans in Belarus, see, for example, Amy Knight, *Beria: Stalin's First Lieutenant* (Princeton, N.J.: Princeton University Press, 1993), p. 122.

55 USSR Central Statistical Administration, *Narodnoe khozyaystvo SSSR v 1984g: statisticheskiy ezhegodnik* (Moscow: Finansy i statistika, 1985), pp. 138, 148.

56 *XXV s'ezd Kommunisticheskaya partii Sovetskogo Soyuza: Stenograficheskiy otchet* (Moscow: Politizdat, 1976), p. 156.

57 At the 24th Party Congress in March 1971, for example, Masherau ended his speech as follows:

Belorussia's working people, like those of all our country, are stirred to wrath and indignation by every revisionist vulgarization of Marxism-Leninism and proletarian internationalism and by attempts to reduce these concepts to the level of empty verbal declarations that are called upon to mask or to excuse narrowly nationalistic or purely selfish interests and aspirations....The right wing revisionists have for all practical purposes united with the avowed anticommunists and anti-Sovieteers. We see this shameful alliance in the pseudoscientific arguments about some kind of "renovation" of Marxism, in the pitiful attempts to portray Leninism as a closed, local phenomenon, and in talk about the so-called pluralism of Marxism, the multiplicity of national models of socialism, etc.

Current Digest of the Soviet Press, *Current Soviet Policies VI: The Documentary Record of the 24th Congress of the Communist Party of the Soviet Union*. Compiled by Richard Bessel. Columbus, Ohio: America Association for the Advancement of Slavic Studies, 1973, p. 69. By any standards the language employed seems strong and demonstrates the commitment of the Belarusian party leader to Marxism–Leninism and his opposition to any deviationism (in this case the Chinese version of Communism).

58 This statement is not to deny the dramatic decline of the Belarusian language in this period, a factor that may be attributable more to official policy in Moscow than any initiative in Minsk.

59 See, for example, Amy Knight, "Pyotr Masherov and the Soviet Leadership: A Study in Kremlinology," *Survey*, Vol. 26, No. 1 (Winter 1982): 167. Knight notes that both leaders had also lost control over the KGB in their respective republics. For a perspective on the changes that occurred in Ukraine in 1972, see Bohdan Krawchenko, ed, *Ukraine After Shelest'*, Edmonton: Canadian Institute of Ukrainian Studies, 1983.

60 After the removal of Nikita S. Khrushchev by a coup d'etat in 1964, a ruling trio eventually emerged in the Soviet Union: Leonid Brezhnev as the party secretary; Aleksey Kosygin as the prime minister; and Nikolay Podgorny (Mykola Pidhorny) as the head of state. By 1973, the first signs that the collective leadership were ending were signified by the fact that Brezhnev's name appeared first in the press. By the time of the 25th Party Congress in 1976, he was clearly the leading figure, and the following year he became the head of state (the formal president). After Kosygin's death in 1980, Brezhnev also added the premiership to his growing list of titles. See, for example, John M. Thompson, *A Vision Unfulfilled: Russia and the Soviet Union in the Twentieth Century* (Toronto: D.C. Heath and Co., 1996), p. 423.

61 Knight, "Pyotr Masherov and the Soviet Leadership," p. 155.

62 Vladimir Yakutov, *Petr Masherov: Khudozhestvenno-dokumental'naya povest'* (Minsk: Rus Belaya, 1992), pp. 250–251.

63 See, for example, Masherau's speech at the 3rd Session of the Congress, in *XXV s'ezd Kommunisticheskoy partii Sovetskogo Soyuza, 24 Fevral'ya-5 Marta 1976 goda: stenograficheskiy otchet*, Vol. 1 (Moscow, Izdatel'stvo politicheskoy literatury, 1976), pp. 154–160.

64 Slavomir Antonovich, "Petr Masherov: 'Ryadom's Brezhnevym," *Respublika*, September 24, 1993, p. 7.

65 Ibid., September 25, 1993, p. 7.

66 Ibid., September 28, 1993, p. 7.

67 P.M. Masherov, *Sovetskaya Belorussiya*, Moscow: Izdatelstvo politicheskoy literatury, 1980, p. 20.

68 Ibid., p. 119. The book also attacks "bureaucratism and formalism," which was surely directed toward the Moscow party leadership. The fact that the book was published in Moscow rather than Minsk assured it of a broad readership.

69 Knight, "Pyotr Masherov and the Soviet Leadership," p. 160.

70 Guthier, "The Belorussians," part 2, p. 275.

71 Calculated from State Committee of the Belorussian SSR for Statistics, *Narodnoe khozyaystvo Belorusskoy SSR v 1989g.* (Minsk: Belarus', 1990), pp. 118–119.

72 Roman Solchanyk, "The Study of the Russian Language in Belorussia," *Radio Liberty Research Bulletin*, RL 30/80, 21 January 1980.

73 The author discusses urbanization in detail in Marples, *Belarus. From Soviet Rule to Nuclear Catastrophe*, pp. 21–23.

Chapter 2

THE ECONOMY: 1986–1996

This chapter examines economic development in Belarus over the course of the decade 1986–1996. Though Belarus was considered relatively successful in terms of industrial development as a Soviet republic, it was ill equipped both for the processes of economic reform and—particularly—for life as an independent state. The decade saw a decline in a number of spheres, such as gross domestic product, labor productivity, and balance of trade. Price rises led to increased wages and very high inflation levels. None of these problems were unique to Belarus in the post-Soviet era, but the country suffered more than most because of its lack of natural resources and its dependence on Russia. The period saw the buildup of debt, more than half of which was owed to Russia. In addition, Belarus also saw a notable demographic decline, which led to dire predictions of the ultimate extinction of the nation. The decade began with an equally catastrophic event, namely the nuclear accident at the Chernobyl plant just south of the Ukrainian border.

THE CHERNOBYL DISASTER

The accident at the fourth reactor of the Chernobyl nuclear power plant on 26 April 1986 has been one of the most heavily researched topics of the Gorbachev period, and its repercussions have continued to affect wide areas of Belarus, Ukraine and Russia. Its significance in the history of Belarus is evident; it has formed a separate epoch as distinct from the pre-Chernobyl era as World War II was from the 1930s. In addition, it marked a definite turning point in the Gorbachev administration. Prior to Chernobyl, the proposal to initiate "glasnost" in all walks of life might have remained largely on paper. With time, however, the ramifications of the "accident made such subterfuge impossible. Chernobyl was directly responsible for the development—albeit gradually—of a more open society, which eventually spread to Belarus, the republic most affected by radioactive fallout. Perhaps its most lasting impact, however, has been on the Belarusian economy.

The extent of radioactive fallout was only revealed officially in the spring of 1989, almost three years after the event. Though some 155,000 people were eventually evacuated from the Belarusian side of the 30-kilometer exclusion zone around the damaged reactor, Moscow for a prolonged period paid little attention to the republic. By 1990, Belarus had received less than 4% of central funds allocated to those suffering from the disaster, as the bulk was allocated to Ukraine and Russia. No major state sponsored campaign to deal with the effects of the accident was developed in the period 1986–89, and the only substantial data base on the actual and potential victims of the disaster in the republic was evidently stolen. Because of the secrecy that surrounded the Chernobyl accident, and the apparent reticence of the Belarusian authorities to take immediate precautionary measures— the distribution of potassium iodide tablets, for example, to reduce the intake of radioactive iodine from the atmosphere—the effects of the accident on the republic were much more serious than might otherwise have been the case. As Foreign Minister Pyotr Krauchanka revealed to the United Nations:

> 70% of the Chernobyl radioisotopes have landed on the Republic. They have contaminated one third of its territory. One fifth of the total population i.e., 2,200,000 people, including almost 800,000 children have become innocent victims of Chernobyl, hostages of delayed hazardous effects of radiation. From 120,000 to 150,000 residents of especially high-risk zones are waiting for their relocation into settlements now under construction in clean zones…The decontamination does not produce expected results. Radionuclides are spreading over the territory of the Republic and threaten to spread beyond. They have been discovered in human tissues also in 'clean' areas.[1]

Studies of some 145,000 residents of Belarus have revealed the growing impact on public health of the radiation released by Chernobyl: a sharp rise in thyroid tumors among children; growing numbers of deaths among clean-up workers; a significant and ostensibly related increase of diabetes among very young children (as young as ten months in some cases); and a discernible rise of leukemia incidence in the republic. The medical problems have been exacerbated by the sluggish progress of resettlement of populations due to the unwillingness of some residents of affected regions to move, administrative red tape, and a shortage of finances. The government only belatedly became occupied with Chernobyl's effects. Ultimately, it issued guidelines on radiation tolerance, allocated benefits for the population living in the contaminated zones, established a State Chernobyl Committee, and set up organizations within institutes and ministries.[2]

Altogether, some 40,000 square kilometers of Belarusian territory was contaminated by Chernobyl, encompassing about 2.2 million people, slightly more than one-fifth of the total population. A decade later, over 1.6 million people continued to live in zones irradiated with more than 1 cu/km^2 in the soil, of whom 298,600 lived in the so-called zone of "voluntary evacuation." They were divided regionally as follows:[3]

1. Minsk Oblast: 192 settlements (towns, villages, and hamlets) with 23,675 people, including 5,245 children.
2. Hrodna Oblast: 151 settlements with 28,381 people, including 6,929 children.
3. Brest Oblast: 166 settlements with 169,497 people, including 48,502 children.
4. Vitsebsk Oblast: 2 settlements with 54 people, including 3 children.
5. Mahileu Oblast: 884 settlements with 146,111 people, including 35,249 people.
6. Homel Oblast: 1,535 settlements, with 1,258,263 people, including 330,663 children.

Thus the main areas affected by radiation today are the Homel, Brest, and Mahileu oblasts. In 1995 the ramifications of Chernobyl, which in the past had eaten up more than 20% of the state budget, were assigned approximately 10% of state expenditure.[4] The result was the virtual cessation of evacuations of people living in contaminated territories, a process rendered controversial from the outset because of the lack of jobs, opportunities and generally poor housing conditions in the new settlements.

The statement can be verified from evacuation figures available from the government. In 1993, the total number of people moved from the radiation zone was 4,410. The following year it fell to 2,778, and in 1995 it dropped once more to 1,442, or 0.1% of the total population living in these regions.[5] If one bears in mind that about 25% of Belarusian land remained contaminated, then the conclusion can be drawn that the government had relegated Chernobyl issues to a matter of secondary importance during the first year of the Lukashenka administration. Though the most pressing evacuations had already been carried out—moving families from the so-called "zone of alienation," in which the soil contained more than 15 cu/km^2 of cesium—a critical situation had developed in the secondary zone: the territory that under government law should have been subjected to evacuation immediately afterward (5–15 curies).

The officials divided the affected regions into four zones according to level of cesium contamination: over 40, 15–40, 5–15, and 1–5 curies of cesium per square kilometer in the soil. Most people lived in the latter zone (1.3 million in 1996 out of the 1.6 million cited above). While numbers fell in the period 1991–95 in almost all zones, the zone of 5–15 curies experienced a rise in its population over this period from 281,300 in 1991 to 298,600 in 1996.[6] The explanation lies in the decomposition of some radionuclides and decontamination measures, expanding the area in the zone (reducing that in the 15–40 curies zone), but it also reflects the return of some residents to their homes and a general reluctance to be moved elsewhere.

The Chernobyl disaster is but one component of the demographic problems in the republic. Most sources acknowledge that it has had a profound impact on the lifestyle and attitudes of the population having children, diet and general nutrition standards, and—less easily discernible—on the health of the population in general. Chernobyl changed the way of life of the population. Thousands of people had received small doses of radiation in addition to the natural background at a time of social and economic decline. Further, initial knowledge about the health effects was restricted by official secrecy. Medical facilities were generally poor. A survey conducted in 1991 with 300 respondents revealed that over 85% of those in the contaminated region aged between 20 and 40 did not plan to increase the size of their families. Among married women with one child, only 7% intended to have further children, while 88% had resolved not to have them. The main reasons cited for not augmenting the family were the potential danger to the child's health of living in irradiated areas (40% of women and 50% of men) and lack of food products (one-third of respondents).[7]

Chernobyl is part of the broader problem of a declining and ageing population that is particularly acute in Belarus. While the number of direct deaths resulting from the accident is not and may never be known, there is no question of the rising morbidity rates, particularly in contaminated regions, and the alarming rise in thyroid gland cancers, particularly among children. The other lasting effect has been the profound psychological impact on lifestyles, the general mistrust of the population for official government statements and actions to alleviate problems arising (and a similar lack of faith in the reports of major international investigations). Chernobyl, ultimately, has changed the demographic picture of Belarus and represents part of a general malaise. It is pertinent therefore to examine briefly the general demographic structure of the republic in the 1986–1996 decade.

DEMOGRAPHIC SITUATION

In 1985, the population of Belarus was 10,028,400, and it reached its peak in 1993 at 10,367,300. Subsequently the country has experienced a population decline. By December 1996, the total population was 10,282,400, a fall of approximately 30,000 from the previous year.[8] The trend appears likely to continue. For each month in 1996, the population continued to fall. There are two basic explanations for the process. First, the decline is a natural one, that is the birth rate is exceeded by the mortality rate. The statement can be qualified further by noting that the number of births has declined quite markedly since 1990, and the number of mortalities has risen sharply. Second, the decline has not been offset by immigration to the republic: people continue to leave—often to seek jobs elsewhere—and the inflow has not compensated fully for the population fall.

In 1990, halfway through the period under examination, the total number of births in the republic was 142,167 and the total mortalities, 109,582. The highest birth rate and lowest mortality rate were in the city of Minsk, in which most of the medical facilities are located. By 1995, the total births had fallen to 101,144, while the mortality rate had risen to 133,775. If one looks at the situation per 1,000 population, then the birth rate had fallen from 13.9 in 1990 to 9.8 in 1995; whereas the mortality rate rose over the same period from 10.7 to 13.0. Regionally, the highest birth rates were in Brest and Hrodna oblasts, and the highest mortality rates occurred in the oblasts of Minsk and Vitsebsk.[9] The figures are disturbing, and there are several possible causes for the natural decline of the population.

The age structure of the population has changed significantly over the past decades. In 1960, for example, 32% of the population were characterized as "young," and 13.6% were of pensionable age. The corresponding figures in 1996 were 23% and 21%.[10] One can distinguish, however, between towns and villages. One in every three rural residents is a pensioner. The younger people gravitate to the towns for jobs or education. As the population ages, more onus is placed on the state to provide medical and social aid. The recent tendency toward a negative population growth rate owes much to the fact that the current trends have taken place during a period of serious economic decline, which has affected adversely the nutrition and general health levels of the population. Not only the elderly have been affected. Infant mortality in Belarus rose from 11.9 per 1,000 births in 1990 to 13.3 in 1995, approximately double the level of the United States.[11] Families, faced with economic hardship, decide not to have children. Real incomes for families with children, particularly single parents, declined drastically during the period after independence.

ECONOMIC DECLINE

Belarus entered a condition of severe economic decline shortly after the declaration of independence. The reality of Belarus dependence on Russia and other countries for energy and raw materials complicated the effort to find solutions based on autonomous economic development. Moreover, low levels of foreign economic investment in Belarus further drove Belarusian politicians toward reintegration with Russia, particularly the Communist or proto-Communist deputies who dominated the Supreme Soviet after the elections of 1990. Belarus was also slow to embark on the road toward market reforms and privatization, and unwilling to try the sort of shock treatment conducted in Poland.

Belarus is a heavily industrialized state, and the most heavily militarized of all the former Soviet republics.[12] Its industrial profile in the immediate aftermath of the dissolution of the USSR was based almost exclusively on military and construction goods to the disadvantage of consumer-oriented production. Thus, Belarusian planners not only had to deal with problems of defense conversion, modernization of existing factories, and industrial pollution; they also had to confront an increasingly dire consumer situation. These problems were greatly exacerbated by the economic trends of the post-Soviet period. Gross output in the economy declined by 14% between 1989 and 1993, most dramatically in agriculture. The real wages of workers also declined to 15% of 1991 levels as a result of dramatic price increases. Exports fell by 36% in volume. Supplies of fuel, raw materials, and other inputs from the states of the CIS contributed to an estimated 43.3% decline in the output of the fuel industry (1991–92), a 15.7% decline in the chemical and oil-chemical complex, a 14.9% drop in ferrous metallurgy, a 17.6% decline in the food industry, and a 9.2% drop in machine-building.[13]

Heavy dependence on Russian and other neighbors' energy resources narrowed the choices available to Belarusian planners. According to three leading energy specialists examining the economic situation in 1993,[14] all fuel-energy resources of Belarus—the small oil supplies in the south; natural gas; peat and firewood; and forestry byproducts—comprised only about 12% of current economic needs. If harnessed, alternative sources of energy (the sun, wind, small rivers, livestock deposits and the like) could at best provide for 10 to 15% of total electricity needs. The republic has no large rivers (even the Dnyapro is relatively narrow in the republic) and enjoys few sunny days. Local supplies of coal and shale also would provide few long-term benefits. The coal is of a low calorific value and its ash content is high. According to the three specialists, energy self-sufficiency would require a total reconstruction of industry, agriculture, and communal services at a cost of billions of rubles and decades of time.[15]

The Chernobyl disaster of April 1986 had serious repercussions that further constrained choices on how to mitigate the energy shortage. By 1993 there was a powerful network of opponents to the construction of nuclear power plants in Belarus. Some of these opponents advocated increased imports of oil and gas instead.[16] But the Russian government's decision to reduce oil supplies to Belarus undermined such a strategy. The issue remained unresolved and largely unaddressed prior to the Lukashenka era. By early 1997, the Belarusian authorities had begun to examine a prospective site for a new station at Dubrovno (Vitsebsk Oblast), close to the present location of the villages Baevo and Zaruby, with the intention to bring a nuclear power plant into operation there by the year 2003.[17] The plan appeared highly optimistic and there was no indication of how such a project might be funded.

Nor did the authorities made a serious effort to transform the command-administrative economy of the Soviet era. A number of laws on privatization and the transition to a free-market economy were promulgated,[18] but many of these decrees remained on paper, and were never implemented. Indeed, the principal advocates of privatization were members of the opposition Belarusian Popular Front (BPF), who criticized the government's insistence on maintaining state control over many enterprises, buildings and land. Between 1991 and 1993, only 308 enterprises were privatized, encompassing just 2.1% of the total workforce. Though the figures were higher in 1994, they are unreliable since in an effort to obtain an IMF loan, factories that were owned and operated entirely by the state were listed as privatized.[19]

State-owned industry accounted for 33% of all factories in 1994, and 35.4% in 1995. They accounted for, respectively, 73.1% and 70% of total output in those years. Private industry accounted for 1.9% of all enterprises and 0.1% of total industrial output in 1994, and 1.4% and 0.2% in 1995. Collective enterprises made up the majority (63.9% in 1994 and 61.9% in 1995) and were divided among leased factories, cooperatives, collective enterprises, economic societies and associations and others. Their share of total industrial output by 1995 was 27.8%. If one examines the critical sectors of the economy in 1994–95, state dominance is even more apparent. State enterprises thus accounted for practically all electricity output in both these years; 65% of all fuel production; 99% of ferrous metallurgy in 1994, and 98.6% in 1995; 92.7% and 90% of chemicals, 77.1% and 72.8% of machine building, and 73.6% and 66.4% in the food industry.[20]

The main spheres of the economy for the expansion of the nonstate sector in these years were the forest and wood-processing industries, light industry, and—to a lesser extent—industrial construction materials. In each case, collective ownership prevailed. By 1996, state-owned enterprises produced about two-thirds of total industrial output of Belarus and nonstate just under one-third, the majority of which were stockholding associations and leased factories.[21] The privatization of industry was developing at a very slow pace, particularly in terms of volume and overall proportion of total output. It was limited to the nonheavy industrial sectors.

The number of joint ventures in the republic in the first post-independence years provides one example of the halfheartedness of the transition from an administrative-command to a proto-capitalist economy. By 1 January 1993, fifty-five countries had embarked on joint ventures in Belarus, led by Poland (with 312 joint ventures), Germany (111), the United States (59), Italy (30), and Austria (23). However, the share in the overall economy remained at less than 1%. Of the 714 joint ventures registered by 1 January 1993, only 164 had actually begun production activities, and foreign businessmen operating in the republic were reportedly acting with a great deal of caution and even reticence, particularly given the government's real (though apparently baseless) concern about the exporting of national treasures as a result of such foreign business operations.[22]

A reported 1309 joint ventures and 452 foreign companies started business in Belarus in the period between August 1991 and July 1994, indicating that almost half of them began operations between January 1993 and July 1994. Over 80% of funds invested in them came from Poland, Germany, Taiwan, USA, Italy, and Canada. Of those wholly owned by foreign businesses, the majority were in Polish and German hands.[23] The summer of 1994 can be considered the heyday of this process as afterward, there was a gradual tightening of laws and official discouragement of private enterprise

On 12 April 1995, Belarus and Russia announced the signing of a monetary union. For Belarusians, the union was seen as a means to alleviate the cost of energy imports. Russia and Belarus would follow a common economic policy, and there would be a free trade (Russian) "ruble zone" on the territory of Belarus. The Belarusian authorities had taken several steps to prop up their ailing currency against the value of the Russian ruble since independence, including a temporary fixed exchange rate of 1:1 and declaring the Belarusian currency the only legal tender in the country in 1993. These measures had failed to halt the skyrocketing costs of imported energy resources from Russia, or the Russian purchase of cheap goods from Belarusian stores, thus causing problems for Belarusian consumers. Though opposed by the chairperson of the National Bank, Stanislau Bahdankevich, the union was accepted by the Belarusian side. Once details were subject to further elaboration in the fall of 1995, however, the Russians rejected the union as economically inexpedient. While many Belarusians had supported the union, the BPF and others had considered the agreement an infringement on the national sovereignty of Belarus.[24] It was in retrospect merely the first of several attempts to unite the weak Belarusian economy with that of the stronger Russian partner.

The slow pace of economic change can be attributed to a number of factors. First, Belarus lacked the international attention and appeal of Russia or Ukraine. This reduced its attractiveness to foreign investors, complicated the efforts of pro-democratic forces in the republic (who could not rely on international pressure for assistance), and heightened Belarusian dependence on an "Eastern" orientation toward economic development. A small republic of 10.3 million people, landlocked, and wedged into Eastern Europe required some publicity to attract foreign investors. Second, Belarus's relative shortage of resources for autonomous development heightened the perception in Minsk that few alternative choices existed to closer economic links with Russia. Third, throughout the period under investigation, the government itself was reluctant to embark on large-scale privatization of industry. This attitude can be elucidated by a closer observation of the economic policies adopted under the Lukashenka government.

THE ECONOMY UNDER LUKASHENKA

The first year of Lukashenka's administration offered a muddled picture. The government lacked any firm direction in economic policy, though in general it adhered to the principles of a market economy as long as Stanislau Bahdankevich retained his position as chairperson of the National Bank of Belarus. Despite some protests against Bahdankevich in the winter of 1994, the government elaborated a program with a goal of financial orthodoxy and the gradual introduction of market reforms. On 12 December, it was announced that prices for bread and milk would be freed, and housing and electricity charges would no longer be subsidized. Government price controls would generally be lifted, monopolies would be reduced, and the budget deficit would be no more than 4% of the gross domestic product. These measures were aimed partly at satisfying the International Monetary Fund (IMF), which promised to provide some $800 million in external aid provided that certain conditions were met.[25]

It proved impossible, however, for the government to adhere to such policies without arousing widespread discontent among the workforce. On 26 January 1995, some 20,000 trade unionists organized a protest in Minsk to demand higher wages to compensate for the price rises. The chairperson of the Federation of Belarusian Trade Unions, Uladzimir Hancharyk, declared that the people had reached their breaking point, as wages were being undermined by rampant inflation.[26] At this time the minimum wage was the equivalent of about $33 per month. At the bottom of the scale were social workers, just below agricultural laborers. Teachers were slightly better off at $58 per month. The highest paid workers were in banking at $129 per month.[27] Real wages, based on purchasing power, declined by over 45% between 1990 and the first quarter of 1995.[28] In the first quarter of 1997, likewise, price rises outpaced wage increases by a factor of three.[29] The workforce of Belarus was being rapidly reduced to impoverishment.

The government faced a recurring problem of meeting wage demands when expenditure consistently exceeded revenue in each budget year. In late 1995, for example, the budget deficit rose sharply when the government authorized, belatedly, about $480 million in subsidies to the agricultural sector. Such measures were self-defeating in that they led directly to suspension of IMF credits.[30] This trend has not only continued, however, but the value of Belarusian exports plummeted in the period 1994–96, while imports remained at former levels. In the latter year, for example, measured in millions of dollars, total exports amounted to $4.8 billion, and imports $8.2 billion; with CIS countries, the corresponding figures were exports $3.2 billion and imports $4 billion.[31] This imbalance remained an acute problem throughout the period under study.

Moreover, foreign investment in the country declined in 1995 to about 20% of the 1991 figure, or about 20 cents per head of population, reportedly the lowest total in Eastern Europe. Clearly foreign investors—in the past the majority hailed from Poland, Germany, and the United States—were reluctant to invest in a country that was politically unstable and in which a plethora of taxes and duties were placed on corporations, including a profit tax, income tax, property tax, value added tax, fuel tax and natural resources tax.[32] Two Western analyses highlighted the basic problems. World Bank representative Christopher Willoughby stated that the main problems in 1995 were currency controls (see below), the slow pace of reforms, and the volatile political climate. The IMF chair, Michel Camdessus, noted that the government had intervened to prop up the Belarusian rubel, that the National Bank had no authority over the exchange rate and credit policy, and that there was a general lack of progress in the sphere of privatization.[33]

The economy continued to contract. The volume of industrial output (GDP), measured in percentages, dropped constantly from 1990 to 1995, and totalled more than 12%. The most pronounced decreases were in the production of ferrous metallurgy, light industry, the food industry, and machinery and metalworking, formerly the most stable facet of the Belarusian economy. Electricity production declined by 19%, and fuel dropped by 43% between 1990 and 1994 (though this sector recovered in 1995).[34] The general trend is clear. An economy that was an integral part of the Soviet planning system had collapsed once that system no longer existed. The gross domestic production per head of population in 1995 was $4,100, a drop of 37% since 1988.[35] In September 1995, Lukashenka obtained the resignation of the chairperson of the National Bank of Belarus, Bahdankevich, the last truly dedicated economic reformer in the administration,[36] thus satisfying critics of the government who had maintained that the president was unable to control the head of the bank.

Bahdankevich's position as central bank chief had become untenable and he feared that the likely alternative to his resignation was arrest and possible imprisonment for libel and defamation (these fears were not far-fetched since this fate awaited his eventual successor, Tamara Vinnikava). The two main reasons for his departure were his longstanding adherence to and propagation of economic reform policies and opposition to monetary union with Russia; and second, the presidential campaign then under way to silence opponents of the government's policies, often through arrest, censorship and intimidation. Bahdankevich's opposition to the proposed monetary union with Russia predated the presidency of Lukashenka. He had also been successful in his policy to make the *zaichyk*, the Belarusian rubel, the legal tender throughout the country. These policies earned him the wrath of factions such as the Pan-Slavic Congress and other groups that supported reunion with Russia in one or another form. In fact once Lukashenka won the presidential election, the dismissal of Bahdankevich was widely expected.[37]

The Bahdankevich period saw some economic accomplishments. On 13 September 1995, he won the agreement of the IMF to the provision of $300 million in standby credit to Belarus. The sum was to be allocated in five tranches, beginning with an immediate issue of $70 million. The agreement was the last official function of the bank chief, and likely the reason why Lukashenka delayed measures to bring about his departure. On the other hand, Bahdankevich had been consistent in his opposition to any form of economic union with Russia, one of the underlying basic goals of the presidency. Economic union had been declared the "prime mandate," with political union an optional second.[38] Bahdankevich subsequently became a leading member of the parliamentary opposition, prior to the dismissal of parliament by the president in November 1996 (see Chapter 5).

Lukashenka's commitment to economic reform was ambivalent at best. By 1996, there were signs that the state was once again starting to reassert its control over several spheres of the economy. On 8 May, for example, when addressing a group of veterans for the Victory Day celebration, the president stated that the government would shortly acquire complete control over the economy, and that banks also would be subject to these changes. Just two weeks later, he put his words into practice by bringing the Inter-Bank Accounting Center under the jurisdiction of the government. Hitherto it had been owned by 16 commercial banks and the central bank. In this same month, Lukashenka's principal economic advisor, Pyotr Kapitula, declared that the government would also keep a firm hand over the exchange rate for the Belarusian rubel, implicitly by using state reserves to prop up its value against the US dollar.[39] For most of 1995 and the first quarter of 1996, the rubel was held at 11,500 to the dollar. From mid-1996 to February 1997, when it was floated freely and there were multiple exchange rates, the rate of exchange soared to 15,500 by the end of 1996, and over the 20,000 mark early in 1997.[40]

In February 1997, the government introduced a unified official exchange rate. By this time hard currency reserves of the National Bank of Belarus had dwindled to less than $10 million, a figure considered insufficient to cover imports for more than a week. The government appears to have backed away from an exchange rate policy that is oriented to the market, though economic experts in Belarus have concurred that to date the government lacks the means to enforce a reduction of the differences in exchange rates between the official rate and that of the black market.[41] One wonders how the National Bank can continue to operate during periods when its reserves have plummeted so low.

Further evidence that the president sought a return to familiar methods of state control surfaced during a meeting of the Cabinet on the harvest, when he demanded the renewal of "socialist competition," and that farmers and combine harvesters who performed well during the harvesting should have their photographs in the major newspapers, thereby replacing the constant pictures of strikers and demonstrators.[42] He also reinstituted the voluntary working Saturday, or *subbotnik*, remarking on television that he would be flying over the country by helicopter to ensure that the various tasks were being carried out. The first such *subbotnik* was greeted with some enthusiasm, particularly in the villages where people could be seen at an early hour sweeping the streets and cleaning windows of cottages.

The president also instituted a protectionist policy in stores. In order to reduce the demand for cheaper imports, it was decreed that at least 75% of the stock of all stores must be manufactured locally. The prices on imported goods were increased by 50%. One of the goals of this decree was to ensure that the accumulating stockpile of home-grown products was lowered.[43] Privatization, much discussed over the past few years, was clearly not a priority by the second year of the Lukashenka government. Symbolically the ministry for privatization did not even have a minister for eighteen months! Inflation was reduced in 1996 partly as a result of unpaid wages to workers in the state sector. Hitherto it had spiralled out of control: 80% in 1991, 2,221% in 1994, and 709% in 1995 (falling to around 90% in 1996). Exports and imports remained oriented toward Russia, which supplied over half of Belarus' energy needs.[44]

UNEMPLOYMENT

Unemployment became an important factor by the mid-1990s, largely as a result of downsizing in industry and the transition of some factories to part-time work. In the period January-November 1996, for example, 436,100 people (11% of the general workforce) were working part time, and of those laid off, more than half received no unemployment benefits. The number of unemployed in 1996 was 1.3 times higher than the previous year, at 256,000 people, with the largest single increase in the city of Minsk (152.2%). The majority of the unemployed were women (63.7%), and the age group most affected was between 20 and 24, which accounted for about one-sixth of all officially registered unemployed. The broader age category of 16–29 years made up 47.8% of the total, and lack of work was particularly acute among graduates of universities, colleges, and technical institutes. Altogether 3.9% of the total labor force was officially unemployed by the end of 1996.[45]

In some areas, unemployment was considerably higher than the republican average. Both cities and villages were equally subject to the worsening situation, though the urban regions inevitably registered much higher totals. On 1 January 1997, for example, 156,700 people were registered as unemployed in the cities, 85.9% of the total, and an increase of 42.6% over the previous year. In the rural localities, the total was 25,800, a rise of 22.3%, and particularly high in Homel Oblast.[46] The situation was exacerbated by the failure of the state sector to pay wages on a regular basis in 1996–97. Correspondingly, the number of people employed also dropped. At the start of the Gorbachev period, in 1985, it stood at 5.12 million, rising slightly to 5.24 million by 1990. Only in the period of independence did the figure fall below 5 million, but by the end of 1996 it had dropped to 4.15 million.[47] The decline of almost one million people in the labor force belied the official unemployment figure (3.9% of the workforce), though the fact that some formerly employed were now pensioners must be taken into consideration.

Unemployment had become an integral part of life in post-Soviet Belarus. The problem did not originate with, but worsened under, the Lukashenka administration.

In the first quarter of 1997, the president announced that unemployment had fallen by about 4,500 people. He gave instructions that no matter how large the enterprise, managers must not simply lay off workers but should set up new areas of work for those facing layoffs. He expressed his wish that employment should fall below the figure of 3% by the end of the year.[48] Such an outcome, at the time of writing, appeared unlikely. Unemployment and underemployment had become characteristics of the Belarusian economy. The contribution of the privatized sector to the GDP was less than 15%, the lowest of all the post-Communist countries. Aside from official figures, the situation was evident to any visitor in 1996–97 who compared business in central Minsk to that in Moscow, Petersburg, or even Kyiv. There was an inherent contradiction between Lukashenka's assurances to the international financial community (especially the IMF and the World Bank) that the country would embark on an economic reform program, and the woeful progress of privatization, foreign investment, and government incentives to businesses, both domestic and foreign.

1996: THE MYTH OF AN ECONOMIC REVIVAL

According to official reports, the Republic of Belarus had begun to recover from its economic decline in 1996. The Lukashenka government was anxious to assure the public that some sectors of the economy had begun to perform well. The dramatic declines in the GDP had reportedly ended, and in fact an increase of 2.6% had been registered in the year 1995. The best performances had been recorded in the forest industry, light industry, and ferrous metallurgy, all sectors of deep decline in past years. On the other hand, the decline had continued in electricity production and fuel output, though these spheres were the exception to the general rule. Over 70% of factories had increased their output. The rise had been higher in the small non-state sector than in state enterprises, though even the latter had recorded a rise in output. Agricultural output had also risen by 2.4%.[49] What had occurred? Do these figures constitute a turn for the better in the Belarusian economy?

The answer is that the revival was an artificial creation. In 1996, for example, even the president acknowledged that warehouse stocks accounted for over half the total output of goods,[50] meaning that official statistics, as in the past, were hardly reliable. Few of the almost overwhelming problems facing the Belarusian economy had been resolved. The balance of payments situation had worsened as a result of import-export disequilibrium and the falling exchange rate for the Belarusian rubel against the dollar and Russian ruble. By the end of 1996, the trade deficit amounted to $1.38 billion, about half of which was comprised of debts to Russia for imports of oil and gas. The fact that a customs union and an agreement to form a Community with Russia had been signed in 1995 and 1996 respectively, had failed thus far to result in two-way trade, according to a Belarusian account.[51]

UNOFFICIAL STATISTICS

Evidence also emerged that official statistics were not merely misleading the public, but were actually distorted. Two sources can be cited, both of which are high-level but extra-government. A sobering analysis of progress in agriculture was offered in a booklet issued on behalf of the Supreme Soviet that had recently been disbanded by the president (see Chapter 5). According to its figures, consumption of basic products in 1996 declined compared to 1995: consumption of meat per head of population from 58 to 54 kilograms; milk and milk products correspondingly from 363 to 350, and potatoes from 185 to 180. The consumption of grain products remained static. In terms of output, that of meat had fallen in these same years from 323,600 tons to 278,900 tons; and grain and grain products from 1.01 million tons to 963,000 tons. Only sugar consumption and production increased in the period 1995–96.[52]

A precipitous and disturbing decline had occurred in the heads of livestock of the various categories. All types of livestock declined in numbers in 1995–96, but if examined over the longer period 1991–96, the extent of the reduction can be better comprehended. In 1991, for example, Belarus had the following livestock totals (thousands of head): large horned 6,200, including 1,699 cows; pigs 3,545; sheep 210; poultry (millions) 291. In 1996, the totals were as follows: large horned 4,035, including 1,309 cows; pigs 2,165; sheep 19; and poultry (millions) 197. Not since the years of early collectivization or the wartime period had there been such a decline in heads of livestock. The gross collection of all agricultural products had declined, including grain and grain-bean products from almost 7 million tons in 1990 to 5.3 million by 1996; potatoes from just under 4 million to 1.7 million; and vegetables from 503,000 tons to 231,00 tons. The grain harvest as measured, Soviet-style, in centners per hectare, had fallen from 26.6 in 1990 to 21.6 in 1996.[53]

One result of this phenomenon of wholesale agricultural collapse was the unavailability of agricultural products to the population. With scarcity, prices became high. By early 1997, prices in Belarus were higher than those in many European countries, and all former Soviet countries with the exception of Russia. The price for chicken, for example, was five times higher than in Poland, and for pork more than double. The agreements between Russia and Ukraine applied customs duties on imported goods from those countries, particularly sugar. The portrait presented here by the parliament was fundamentally different from the official version offered by the Lukashenka government, Indeed it indicated a wholesale and worrying decline in agriculture thanks to the confusion of customs arrangements, a reduction in purchasing power of farmers (many of whom could no longer afford to purchase tractors and other agricultural machinery), their inability to apply mineral goods to the soil (1.5 million tons were applied in 1990; 620,000 in 1996), and other factors.

A second analysis was offered by Henadz Karpenka, chairperson of the National Economic Council and a corresponding member of the Belarusian Academy of Sciences. In an article that accused the government of outright lies in its economic statistics, he pointed out that in world economics there is a direct correlation between the rise in output and the production and use of electricity. In Belarus, however, the volume of output of industrial goods had allegedly risen at a time when output of electricity had declined. The government had concealed the latter fact by measuring output in millions of rubels for the first quarters of 1996 and 1997 without taking into account the decline in the value of the rubel. In short, the figures, as measured in this fashion were meaningless. Actual output of electricity had declined from 7.1 billion kilowatt /hours in the first quarter of 1996 to 6.8 billion in the same period of 1997. Other types of energy production had also seen reductions in output: reprocessed oil by 21%; benzine by 4%; diesel fuel by 16%; mazut (black oil) by 24%.[54]

A second contradiction had occurred in agricultural statistics. According to official figures, output of milk had risen by 3% (first quarter of 1997), while the heads of cattle had fallen by 4%. Karpenka pointed out many such paradoxes. However, the true indicator of living standards remained the purchasing power of the population. Official results for 1997 again painted an optimistic picture, with a 10% rise in GDP, bolstered by an increase of 17.6% in industry. Once again, however, the statistics were misleading. Imports continued to outpace exports and the annual budget deficit had continued to rise. By the spring of 1998, over 80% of all industrial enterprises in Belarus were not in a position to pay off their debts, and were for all intents and purposes bankrupt.[55] Because of continuing price rises, real purchasing power was being continually reduced, particularly for pensioners. As a result of the imbalances in the economy, the Belarusian currency dropped sharply against the dollar in March 1998, rising from just over 30,000 to 70,000 in two weeks at a time when the president was out of the country.[56] Upon his return, he demanded that the rates be fixed at their former levels, and ordered that concomitant food price rises be nullified, threatening the chairman of the National Bank with dismissal.[57] Though the government maintained that the "run" on the currency was planned by outside agencies or "criminal elements", in reality the weakness of the currency only reflected the integral shortcomings of Belarusian industry and agriculture, and an all-pervasive dependence on Russian capital within the republic's banking system. There was no "economic miracle" in Belarus. On the contrary, government policies were causing an acceleration of the decline.

ECONOMIC FUTURE

On the other hand, Belarus was not facing economic collapse. Speculation that the Lukashenka government could eventually fall because of the failure of the economy appeared to be far-fetched. The government had a limited vision, perceiving union with Russia as the solution to its economic ailments rather than the sort of economic reforms conducted in neighboring Poland (or, for that matter, in Russia itself), and generally there was little justification for the title of a recent article in a Belarusian economic journal entitled "stabilization of the instability."[58] The problems must be put into perspective. Officially Belarus performed slightly better than average among the newly independent states of the former Soviet Union (according to government statistics) in 1996, behind Turkmenistan, Uzbekistan, and Kyrgyzstan, but ahead of Kazakhstan, Ukraine, Azerbaidzhan, and even Russia. However, we have already noted the discrepancies in official statistics, especially when measured in terms of GDP over the previous year. There was little correlation between the figures and the increasingly grim realities for the majority of citizens.

Critical dilemmas remain in the late 1990s, from the balance of payments deficit to the continuing repercussions of the Chernobyl accident. Further, Belarus has been widely regarded as a difficult place to do business, partly because of the frequency with which laws are introduced and amended, but also because of the development of a repressive political climate. Belarus has experienced many of the problems of the first years of capitalism, but few of the benefits. The government has not to date provided a climate conducive to the development of small businesses, foreign companies, or even joint ventures. Its economic correctives have been largely superficial measures imposed centrally—such as the rubel-dollar exchange rate or the output of goods based on storage from previous years. Its economy is directed almost exclusively toward the east, despite some efforts by Poles, Germans, and Americans to rectify the situation. Finally the economic difficulties have exacerbated (if they did not initially create) a demographic crisis: a population decline, high infant mortality rates, and a reduction of the lifespan of the population, particularly that of males. Chernobyl was not the only reason for a general pessimism about the future evident in many Belarusian circles in the 1990s.

1   Byelorussian Soviet Socialist Republic (BSSR), Mission to the United Nations, "Statement by Pyotr K. Krauchanka, Minister for Foreign Affairs of the Byelorussian SSR, on agenda item 14 'Report of the International Atomic Energy Agency,'" at the 45th session of the United Nations General Assembly, New York, 23 October 1990.

2   See Marples, *Belarus: From Soviet Rule to Nuclear Catastrophe*, Chs. 3 and 4.

3   L.P. Shakhot'ko, *Naselenie Respubliki Belarus' v kontse XXv* (Minsk: Scientific-Research Institute of Statistics with the Ministry of Statistics of the Republic of Belarus, 1996), p. 153.

4   Mikola Dziabola, "Inflation Programmed into New Budget," *Belarusian Review*, Vol. 7, No. 1 (Spring 1995): 7.

5   Shakhot'ko, *Naselenie Respubliki Belarus'*, p. 152.

6   Ibid., p. 155.

7   Shakhot'ko, *Naselenie Respubliki Belarus'*, p. 161.

8   *Statisticheskiy byuleten'*, No. 12 (1996): 27.

9   *Meditsinskie novosti*, No. 4 (1997): 27.

10 Shakhot'ko, *Naselenie Respubliki Belarus'*, pp. 14–15.

11 *Meditsinskie novosti*, No. 4 (1997): 27.

12 Zaprudnik, *Belarus: At A Crossroads in History*, pp. 206–208.

13 Vladimir Shimov and Yakub Aleksandrovich, "Traektoriya vo vremeni: perspektivy ekonomiki Belarusi." *Belaruskaya dumka*, Vol. 1, No. 4 (April 1993): 14–15.

14 Aleksandr Mikhalevich, Director of the Institute for Problems of Energetics, Academy of Sciences, Republic of Belarus; Fedor Molochko, Director of the Belarusian Thermal Energy Institute; and Andrei Stavrov, Director of the Republican Scientific-Educational and Information Center for Problems of Radiation Safety, Energetics and Radio-ecological Education, Administration Department, Council of Ministers, Republic of Belarus.

15 Aleksandr Mikhalevich, Fyodor Molochko, and Andrey Stavrov, "I okunetsya Belarus' vo t'mu, esli my vovremya nerazberyomsya, v kakom polozhenii nakhoditsya nasha energetika, chto nuzhno sdelat' rukovodtsvu respubliki, chtoby Belarus' izbezhala energeticheskogo krizisa," *Narodnaya hazeta*, 31 March 1993.

16 Yu. Voronezhtsev, "Nyeuzhto odnoy katastrofy malo? ili Nuzhny i Belarus AES?," *Belaruskaya dumka*, No. 4 (April 1993): 1–4.

17 *Argumenty i fakty v Belarusi*, No. 1, 1997, p. 1.

18 For example, "The Basic Principles of Transition of Belarus to a Free-Market Economy," October 13, 1990; and "Basic Principles of Denationalization and Privatization of the Economy of Belarus," 28 May 1991.

19 Tatiana Mamenok, "Privatisation Slow and Erratic," *Minsk Economic News*, No. 21 (November 1996): 5.

20 *Promyshlennost' Republiki Belarus': statisticheskiy sbornik* (Minsk, 1996), pp. 18–20.

21 *Natsyyanal'naya ekanamichnaya hazeta*, No. 6, February 1997, p. 18

22 Leonid Shchukin, "Joint Ventures," *Minsk Economic News*, No. 4, April 1993, p. 4. The lack of major political change was evident at this time to any visitor to Minsk. In fact, the entire problem was aptly symbolized in Independence Square, the vast and largely empty center of Minsk, where a huge statue of Lenin stands amid government buildings. By 1997, however, a number of foreign enterprises had established themselves in the Belarusian capital, headed by the McDonald's restaurant chain, which had established three outlets, including one in the city center. A Ford plant also began operations in Belarus in August.

23   Larisa Bolotnikova, "Investment Trends in Belarus," *Minsk Economic News*, No. 5 (March 1995): 2.

24   See, for example, Ustina Markus, "The Russian-Belarusian Monetary Union," *RFE/RL Research Report*, Vol. 3, No. 20, 20 May 1994, pp. 28–32.

25   Edward Lucas, "Belarus Out of the Slow Lane," *Belarusian Review*, Vol. 6, No. 4 (Winter 1994/95): 12.

26   Reuters, 26 January 1995.

27   Knight-Ridder, 17 November 1995; OMRI Daily Report, 10 October 1995.

28   V.I. Halubovich, ed., *Ekanamichnaya historyya Belarusi* (Minsk: NKF "Ekaperspektyva", 1996), p. 424.

29   "Belarus Summary Statistics," *Belapan*, 21–27 May 1997, p. 24.

30   OMRI Daily Report, 27 March 1996.

31   *Statisticheskiy byuleten'*, No. 12 (1996): 37.

32   Reuters, 21 May 1996; and Larisa Bolotnikova, "Investment Trends in Belarus," *Minsk Economic News*, No. 5, March 1995, p. 2.

33   Reuters, 27 June 1996; OMRI Daily Report, 19 December 1995.

34   *Statisticheskiy byuleten'*, No. 12, 1996, pp. 103–106.

35   Jerzy Kleer, "Bialoruska gospodarka: Droga do Moskwy," *Wprost*, 12 April 1997, pp. 49–50.

36   Reuters, 15 September 1995.

37   Oxford Analytica Daily Brief, 27 September 1995.

38   Ibid.

39   OMRI Daily Report, 9 May 1996; Reuters, 21 May 1996.

40   "Belarus Summary Statistics," *Belapan*, 21–27 May 1997, p. 24.

41   "Balance of Payments and Foreign Exchange in Belarus," *Belapan*, 23–29 July 1997, pp. 15–16.

42   Reuters, 29 July 1996.

43   ITAR-TASS, 27 August 1996.

44   Kleer, "Bialoruska gospodarka," pp. 49–50.

45   "Zanyatost' naseleniya i bezrabotitsa v Belarusi," *Belapan*, 24 February-4 March 1997, pp. 21–23.

46   Ibid., p. 24.

47   *Statisticheskiy byuleten'*, No. 12 (1996): 27.

48   *Radio Minsk*, 30 April 1997.

49   *Natsyyanal'naya ekanamichnaya hazeta*, No. 6, February 1997, p. 18.

50   *Radio Minsk*, 30 April 1997.

51   *Natsyyanal'naya ekanamichnaya hazeta*, No. 6, February 1997, p. 21.

52   Supreme Soviet of the Republic of Belarus of the 13th session, *Sostoyanie i puti vykhoda agropromyshlennogo kompleksa iz krizisa: Materialy tret'ego sobraniya deputatov* (Minsk, February 1997), pp. 13–14.

53   Ibid., pp. 14–16, & ff.

54   Gennadiy Karpenko, "Sekrety 'belorusskogo ekonomicheskogo chuda', ili Obyknovennaya lozh?" *Narodnaya volya*, 7 June 1997, p. 2.

55   *Natsional'naya ekonomicheskaya gazeta*, No. 6, February 1998, p. 7.

56   *Ibid.*, No. 12, March 1998, p. 1.

57   *Sovetskaya Belorussiya*, 19 March 1998, p. 1.

58   Leonid Zaiko, "Nelaskovyy may: stabilizatsiya nestabil'nosti," *Natsyyal'naya ekanamichnaya hazeta*, No. 28, February 1996, p. 27.

Chapter 3

THE DEVELOPING POLITICAL CONFLICT

The advent of the Gorbachev administration did not presage dramatic changes for Belarus until the late 1980s. The events of that period occurred largely as a result of reforms undertaken in Moscow, particularly after the 19th Party Conference of the CC CPSU in the summer of 1988. The policies of glasnost and perestroyka did, however, eventually have a profound impact on the republic, as elsewhere. The geographical location and historical background of Belarus—in both cases linked to the Baltic states—ensured that it could not remain immune to the processes of destalinization, historical reassessment, and revived public opinion that were taking place in the USSR, and in Lithuania in particular. The result was the first attempt in Belarus to form a public association that was widely perceived to be hostile to the Communist Party of Belarus (though Communists were included in its ranks), and was an organization seeking to reestablish the Revival movement of the 1920s: this was the Belarusian Popular Front, which today remains the most significant opposition political party. How was this party founded and what were its aims?

THE BELARUSIAN POPULAR FRONT

The Popular Front was created in the Belarusian SSR in the Fall of 1988, despite official attempts to suppress it, or denigrate it through the publication of scurrilous articles.[1] It emerged as an informal association called "Martyrolog of Belarus" with some 200 members dedicated to the victims of Stalinism (see below). In October 1988 the association founded an Initiative Group of the Popular Front of Belarus, which was then renamed the "Renewal" Belarusian Popular Front for Perestroyka.[2] Its chief foothold was in the city of Minsk, and from the outset the party found it difficult to penetrate the countryside. This was a result of its leadership and domination by the intelligentsia: in fact, both the Communist Party and the BPF represented sections of the Belarusian intellectual elite and both could claim to represent the historical traditions of the "nation." The former could claim roots in the former Russian Empire and the continuing Soviet period, having achieved great national unity at times of crisis, such as the German occupation of Belarus; while the latter was devoted to "restoring" the national heritage of the country, submerged or lost during the period of Russian/Soviet domination. In short, the emergence of the BPF from the first was taken very seriously by the party hierarchy and regarded as a potential threat to its control. Under the new circumstances of glasnost and the transformation of the state economy along market lines, this threat had become pervasive.

Because of harassment at home, the Front held its founding congress in Vilnius, Lithuania on 24–25 June 1989. Of the more than 400 delegates, about 14% were Communist Party members and almost three-quarters of attendees were Belarusians. The BPF declared its intention to form an umbrella group—the Belarusian Popular Front *Adradzhenie*—for different interests: ecological, cultural, and civic. The archeologist Zyanon Paznyak delivered the main address, in which he asserted his belief that Belarus was facing "genocide" and "ethnocide" at the hands of the Soviet regime. A 55-member assembly was appointed, headed by Paznyak, M. Tkachau, and Yu. Khadyka. The BPF announced its goals to establish popular authority and the rebirth of the Belarusian nation.[3]

The leader of the BPF, Zyanon Paznyak, was born on 24 April 1944 in the Vilna region. His grandfather, a leader of the Belarusian Christian Democratic party, was arrested and murdered by the Soviet regime after the Soviet annexation of Vilnius in 1939. His father was recruited into the Red Army and died in December 1944. "Coming from such a family," he recounts in a 1997 interview, "I could not accept Communism." In the 1960s he had been expelled from the Institute of Theater and Art in Minsk, following a rumor that he had wanted to see Communists "hanged from a post." Working on a doctorate in Minsk on the activities of the Belarusian theater in the early 20th century, he was subjected to constant harassment by the KGB for his "independent thinking," and eventually defended the thesis in Leningrad in 1981. Subsequently he pursued his "other profession," that of a historian and archeologist at the Institute of Belarusian History in the Belarusian Academy of Sciences.[4]

Paznyak became the leader of the BPF, in his own words, because he was "quite well known" and "had no choice." He would have preferred, he remarks, to have pursued scholarly work, particularly poetry, but decided to enter an arena in which morality is not often favored. Neither the BPF nor he personally, he emphasizes, are extremists. The BPF has combined in its program the concepts of Christian Democracy and conservatism. Paznyak is a Catholic who believes that everything stems from faith. The observer can make his own deductions on Paznyak's character, but it appears that his outlook has been conditioned by the tragic background of his family, his association with Vilna, a lost city for Belarus, and by a hatred for Communism that has been equated closely with the actions of Russians. At least, when referring to the Soviet regime, the word "Moscow" enters the text very frequently. Paznyak's writings also have a tendency toward hyperbole, particularly when he makes comments on the persecution of Belarusians in the past under the Soviet regime. He was reelected leader of the BPF in the summer of 1997 despite living in exile, perhaps because, as he states, "I have no cardinal political errors on my conscience and that is probably the reason why I have endured."[5]

Official reaction to the formation of the BPF was hostile. According to the Communist authorities in Minsk, the BPF Congress lacked a basic program and had been, by and large, boycotted by major figures in Belarusian cultural society, such as the well known writers Ales Adamovich ("he sent only a brief telegram") and Vasil Bykau, who was visiting Spain at the time.[6] In a veritable tour de force of political propaganda and muddled history, one Minsk newspaper tried to brand the Front as pro-Hitler, by focusing on its celebration of the 72nd anniversary of the establishment of the Belarusian National Republic in March 1918. The BNR, it was held, embraced bourgeois principles, and gave rise to fascist supporters. One of its front pages of March 1990 thus carried the slogans: "No to the enemies of the people! No to the provocateurs! No to the nationalists! Yes to a Soviet socialist motherland!"[7] Such propaganda—including the slanderous film *Children of the Lie*, which equated the BPF directly with the Nazis—revealed the paranoia of the authorities rather than the intentions of the BPF. Clearly there were fears that the BPF had close links with the Lithuanian Sajudis and constituted a serious threat to the Communist Party establishment. But what were the reasons for the BPF's formation, and how did the organization[8] perceive its role in the Soviet state?

In an illuminating article concerning the historical path to Belarusian statehood, Michael Urban and Jan Zaprudnik argue that the formation of the BPF derived from three major events:[9]

1. The language question, which also incorporates Belarusian culture and education, and came to the fore as early as December 1986.
2. The discovery of the executed victims at the Kurapaty Forest, near Minsk by archeologist Zyanon Paznyak, the future leader of the BPF.
3. The impact and effects of the Chernobyl disaster of April 1986 on Belarus.

We will examine the first two issues in turn, as they form crucial markers in the development of democratic processes and national consciousness in the country (on the repercussions of Chernobyl, see Chapter 2). Each issue in its own way reflected badly upon the former Communist regime, and consequently upon those who initially inherited its mantle, namely the Council of Ministers and the conservative bloc of parties within the parliament. Each served as a catalyst of change in the republic and undermined the authority of the ruling elite, and as the facts of such traumatic events as Kurapaty and Chernobyl were revealed, they made it more difficult for the leadership to maintain its links with the former Soviet state. In reality, the significance of these questions outweighed that of the BPF as a political party, because their impact was upon the national consciousness of all Belarusians. Ultimately, the message appeared plain: namely that given the occurrence of such catastrophes that have occurred largely from "outside sources," closer integration with Russia and maintenance of former Soviet traditions would be inexpedient and even disastrous.

THE LANGUAGE ISSUE

The population of Belarus has been subject to high levels of linguistic Russification. Russification was officially introduced in the Stalin period and by the mid-1970s, in the ninety-five cities of the republic, not a single Belarusian school remained. A similar pattern prevailed in the 117 rayon centers, despite the fact that Belarusians at this time made up over 71% of the urban population, and about 80% of the republican population. The situation in the press was only somewhat different, as six of eleven newspapers appeared in the native language; but their circulation figures were only 10% that of Russian-language newspapers. In 1984, only some 5% of journals in circulation were in Belarusian. Indeed, at that time, only about one-third of the total population spoke the native language in their daily life, and these were concentrated disproportionately among rural inhabitants over the age of 35–40.[10]

Not surprisingly in light of these data, Belarusians in 1984 were ranked in last place (15th) of the Soviet nationalities in the percentage of people residing in their national republic who retained the capacity to speak their native language. The figure for Belarusians was 74.2%, compared to 99.9% for Russians, 82.8% for Ukrainians, 85.9% for a stateless nationality like the Tatars, and 76.5% for the Udmurts, who occupied an "autonomous region."[11] The relatively small size of the Belarusian population rendered this problem of low language retention more acute than it would be for a large nation, and raised questions about the extinction of the national language altogether.

This dilemma owes as much to trends in urbanization as it does to the Soviet regime's language policy. While all republics of the former Soviet Union had been subject to rapid urbanization during the past sixty years, Belarus experienced an exceptional pattern in this regard. The extraordinary pace of large-city urbanization at the expense of small towns and rural settlements, and the domination of the republic by a single large city (Minsk), have accelerated and intensified the impact of Russification policies. Thus by 1977, the number of pensioners in rural settlements was greater than the number of children, a trend that was increasing each year more markedly than in its neighbor Slavic states of the USSR. As the young people flocked to the cities they invariably found themselves in large, multi-national work collectives with communication solely in the Russian language.[12]

Moreover, whereas all the large cities experienced rapid growth in the 1970s and 1980s, the city of Minsk grew much faster than any other center, and acquired a dominance over the rest of the republic that has left a demographical imbalance not common in other republics. In brief, Minsk, as capital of the BSSR, was the focus and center of virtually all cultural and political activities of the republic in addition to being the major economic center. Simultaneously, the total dominance of the primate city also led to the near extinction of the native language in Minsk.

Between 1959 and 1973 the population of Minsk grew by 104%, compared to an average urban population growth in the republic of 50%. By 1973, almost a quarter of the urban population of the BSSR was concentrated in Minsk. The city at this time accounted for one-third of industrial production; and 58% of all students enrolled at higher educational institutions. The situation has remained unchanged with time. In 1979, the city of Minsk accounted for 13.2% of the total population of the republic, and 24.0% of the urban population. The respective figures for 1989 were 15.8% and 24.1%, at which time Minsk's population was 1.6 million, three times higher than Homel, its closest rival in population. Minsk is located in the center of the republic and on trade routes,[13] and has the added, though somewhat dubious, status today of being the capital of the Commonwealth of Independent States. Thus it is likely to remain a magnet for new migrants from the countryside and even from other cities. The question arises as to why it should also be the focal point of Russian influence in the republic.

The answer lies both in official policy and history. Russians (and previously the Jewish population) have traditionally concentrated in the cities of Belarus, whereas the native population have been rural dwellers. In some cities, such as Mahileu, the proximity to the Russian border has militated against language retention. Since the Stalinist period, there have also been systematic attempts to eliminate the Belarusian language as a means of communication. As the languages are similar, Belarusian migrants from the countryside soon adopted Russian, often as their native language, and rapidly became assimilated into the host culture, i.e., a Russian-speaking culture dominated by the traditions of the Russian nation. While as recently as 1985, one scholar could declare that in Belarus "the village remains a comparatively solid carrier of the traditional culture in its folkloric and ethnographic form" (G.I. Kasperovich), the village was already becoming a lost world: one of declining population, and lacking in basic amenities such as stores, medical dispensaries and hospitals. The villages were even beginning to disappear completely as the older generation passed away. In short, if left to the villages alone, the national culture would not survive. Thus the development and spread of a distinctive Belarusian national culture would have to be centered in urban settlements that form the focus of republican life.

Is it possible for the development of a national consciousness and culture to occur without the use of the native language? This question has long concerned those with affection for the Belarusian language and culture. One recalls, for example, that the aristocracy of the Russian Empire spoke French until the late 19th century, just as Indian nationalists adopted many of the customs and some of the culture of their British rulers without any apparent dampening of national consciousness. These analogies, however, may be misplaced. For Belarus, national development without the native language, especially under the shadow of a much larger Slavic neighbor with a lengthy historical tradition as an empire, was virtually impossible. As Belarusians in urban centers changed to Russian language usage, they were on the road to complete assimilation.

ATTEMPTS TO RESTRICT RUSSIFICATION

Taking advantage of the opportunities afforded by perestroyka and glasnost, twenty-eight Belarusian writers[14] dispatched a remarkable open letter to Mikhail Gorbachev, on 15 December 1986 in which they exposed in great detail the Russification of Belarus since the 1930s. Citing the example of book publications, the authors pointed out the complete dominance of Russian language publications in recent years. Cultural and cinematography books in Belarusian were no longer being printed, whereas the percentage of art books being published in Russian had increased from 89.9% in 1981 to 95.3% in 1984. In government institutions and the workplace, Belarusian was practically nonexistent. The authors therefore asked General Secretary Gorbachev to reinstate the language in party, state, and local government organs in the republic; to establish a compulsory leaving examination in Belarusian language and literature in secondary schools; and an examination in the language for students prior to entry into all institutes of higher education. A list of journals which should be published in Belarusian was included in an appendix, as was a demand that Belarusian television should be broadcast entirely in the national language.[15]

Other scholars, such as A. Smalenski and Adam Maldzis, followed later with exposes that revealed the extent of both linguistic and cultural decline. By the end of the decade, there appeared to be broad agreement among many scholars that a greater public emphasis on national culture, national heritage, and Belarusian history was required, through clubs, circles, literary and dramatic societies, along with "days of Belarusian language and literature, culture and art." On 4 June 1989 the Frantsishak Skaryna Society of the Belarusian Language held its founding congress, in Minsk and on 26 January 1990 the Supreme Soviet adopted a law "Concerning languages in the BSSR." On 24–31 May, the Belarusian State University co-sponsored an international seminar in Minsk entitled "Belarusian Language, Literature, and Culture in the Context of World, Languages, Literatures, and Cultures.[16] The process perhaps culminated in September 1990 when the government sanctioned a national program on the development of the Belarusian language and the languages of other nationalities in the BSSR, thereby ratifying a decree earlier in the year that established Belarusian as the state language of the republic.[17]

Public discussions in newspapers, journals, and the electronic media also raised the level of popular awareness of the dilemma. The language issue became a debating point. Critics began to accuse the Soviet regime of deliberately stifling the native language and of being responsible for the low levels of national consciousness among the population. Partly as a result, young students began to search for the roots of their culture and discussions of language became the norm rather than the exception, even penetrating such formerly inaccessible vehicles as the party's theoretical organ *Kommunist Belorussii*. The intellectual leadership of the Belarusian state was also becoming more effective, as was evident in official measures to promote the national language: its usage by prominent officials at public functions; the establishment of a television station and several radio stations in Belarusian; street and metro signs; and so on.

It is natural that independence for Belarus would result in highly charged discussions about national identity and national interest, and that this would trigger a search for national and cultural distinctiveness. It is also natural that such a search would be initiated and led from within the intelligentsia. But if this were to penetrate the middle and lower levels of the population, it would have to confront a widespread mind-set that was the product of decades of intense Russification.

The process of Belarusian nation-building was clearly difficult from the outset. But the issues were at least joined at the level of the political elite and the intelligentsia. Moreover, the revival of national consciousness in the era of perestroyka was possible because of a perceived sympathy in Moscow at the level of the higher party leadership for such changes. The period resembled the 1920s when Lenin first allowed the republics to develop systems that were "national in culture, socialist in content." Paradoxically, once the support from the "center" ended, i.e., the USSR collapsed, there was no longer any significant support for the national awakening. The gains in cultural development during the Gorbachev period were thus not brought to their natural fruition during the period of independence. It is one of the unique features of Belarus that the ruling elite embarked on a conscious negation of its own culture and past during the period of independence, and particularly after 1994.

THE KURAPATY REVELATIONS

The rediscovery by Zyanon Paznyak of a reported 500 mass graves in the Kurapaty Forest near Minsk in the spring of 1988 did more to raise the national consciousness of the republic than any other event of the Gorbachev period.[18] It occurred during a time of official destalinization in the USSR, which enabled the Belarusians to organize a mass meeting to commemorate Stalin's victims without fear of dispersal. For the authorities, this became an embarrassment because the tone of the meeting questioned the legitimacy of Soviet policy toward Belarus (the Belarusian SSR), and pointed out that the perpetrators of the atrocity were still at large. A local geologist described the situation as follows:

> Stalin was the chief conductor of the orchestra and he used the Commissariat of Internal Affairs, which was given unlimited powers. This place [Kurapaty] was a school for executioners and sadists. And they are still alive today. I even saw one of them at this meeting, he stood at the perimeter of the crowd. He told me that he could use some tanks. Unfortunately there are no books about these criminals…we need proper documentation of Stalin's crimes.[19]

The authorities were not anxious to reveal the real nature of what had occurred at Kurapaty. Under the pressure of Paznyak's revelations, in the summer of 1988, the Belarusian authorities established a Government Commission to investigate the discovered graves. It was headed by Deputy

Chairman of the Council of Ministers, N.N. Mazay, and included the Chief Prosecutor of the republic, H.S. Tarnauski. Its composition was varied. It included representatives of the Minsk oblast and city governments, former partisans and war heroes, military commissars, and some scholars and artists. However, its makeup was dominated by what might be termed "conservatives" from the nomenklatura. Of the twenty-one officially listed members, only three appeared to be relatively independent of the administration. Moreover, the inclusion of E.I. Shyrkouski, the First Deputy Chairman of the Belarusian KGB—notwithstanding the inclusion of Paznyak, who had first made the discovery—was an indication that the authorities were not anxious to uncover the full extent of the executions and that from the outset the inquiry was of a limited nature. The Commission expressed its desire, however, to work with scholars from the Academy of Sciences, particularly archeologists and historians.[20]

Its conclusions were terse, and barely skimmed the surface of an horrific atrocity. It established that in an area of about thirty hectares, it had come across 510 assumed burial places. The bodies were exhumed by noted archeologists, criminologists and doctors, and the fragments of over 3,000 items of personal belongings were examined by thirty-eight legal experts. The Institute of Legal Expertise of the BSSR Ministry of Justice permitted its ballistic experts to examine cartridges and bullets, fragments of shoes and coins, remains of clothing and other personal effects. Experts from the BSSR Trading and Industrial Chamber perused items that had some sort of commodity value, while the Academy of Sciences conducted "laser analysis" of certain items. Altogether there had been exhumed the bones of "not less than 356 persons." Most of them had evidently died with a single shot to the back of the head, with bullets that were manufactured in the period 1928 to 1939.

Clothing and shoes indicated to the Commission's experts that the social makeup of those executed was broad. Each mass grave contained 50–60 people, which led the Commission to declare that in the forest there must be at least 30,000 buried.[21] It was not possible, its report stated, to establish a more precise figure at that time. Fifty-five witnesses had testified to shootings in 1937, and that part of the forest in which burials had been carried out had been surrounded by a high fence. The fence had been demolished and the forest destroyed by the German invaders. Trees had been replanted over the burial grounds after the war, as the age of the trees (35 to 46 years) testified.[22] The names of the dead were not recorded, declared the Commission report, because it was standard practice for NKVD organs not to provide information about the location of the executions and the burial of the corpses. However, there was no doubt expressed as to the perpetrators of the crime: the NKVD had conducted mass executions of Soviet citizens in the years 1937 to 1941.

The government subsequently erected a monument to the victims at Kurapaty. It is not a very impressive affair and the government clearly did not dig deep into its coffers to finance it. It stands by the roadside at one of the entrances to the forest. A further study was commissioned, and the *Belorusskaya Sovetskaya Entsiklopediya* was asked to produce a special issue commemorating the event, and the memory of those who were repressed in the 1930s to the 1950s. From the start, however, there were several problems with the investigation, in addition to the partisan nature of its composition. First, the time period allotted to an investigation of this nature was clearly inadequate. A study of the investigation of one of the largest mass murders in history had been completed in six months. Not one executioner or victim had been named. There were evident discrepancies in the dating of trees. Finally, there was a discernible anxiety on the part of the government to put the event behind them, to complete the report as quickly as possible, provide a monument and thereafter to maintain the documentation in closed archives. Kurapaty was thus perceived and feared as a potential unifying factor for Belarusians against Soviet authority, and as a catalyst for the development of a long dormant national consciousness.

While more cautious old guard members have sought a middle ground concerning the revelations about Kurapaty, the most determined assaults on the Commission report emanated from the Communist side, and particularly from those who served in the partisans in the Great Patriotic War. One Commission member, Maryya Barysava-Osipava, openly dissented from the official report, and refused to sign the document. In her view, the mass executions had been conducted not by the NKVD, but by the German invaders and their supporters, a fact of which she was aware as a member of the underground group in occupied Minsk. The underground had infiltrated the Minsk police forces (under German administration) and uncovered executions at the Minsk prison. The victims, she stated, were in fact not Belarusians, but Jews from Germany and Poland, who were being taken to "the execution grounds at Zelenyi Lug." Zelyony Luh was a former village located just over a mile from today's Kurapaty Forest. Moreover, declared Barysava-Osipava, there was no forest at this location during the war years. She maintained also that evidence that might suggest Nazi involvement in the killings was confiscated by members of the Commission.[23]

The Commission's findings were also criticized by the former commander of a partisan unit, I. Kh. Zaharodnik, based on a personal investigation motivated by anger at the accusations against the NKVD. He argued first that no bullets of 1939 make could have been used by the NKVD in the time period indicated, since such bullets took at least eighteen months for the passage from manufacture to usage. Thus bullets made in 1939 could not have been put into use until 1941. Rather the Germans and local police had used Soviet weapons and ammunition for their executions. The NKVD did have an execution place, but within Minsk itself. He also states that there was no forest at Kurapaty during the war years. Even the exhumations were preplanned, he declared. When a gasline was constructed in the forest region, it was laid out in such a way as to circumvent the mass graves, and thus someone must have already known about their presence. The public had been deceived over Kurapaty. The social composition of the victims, in his view, was varied precisely because the victims were refugees from the western regions of Belarus and Poland, who had fallen into the hands of the Germans.[24]

Both these attempted refutations of the mass executions were published in a hardline Minsk Communist newspaper. They have not received serious attention from historians, but they did raise some important points. Their basic premise is that the real enemy of the Belarusians in the 1940s was not Stalin's NKVD, but the German Nazis. Without such an enemy, the Communist leadership of the republic would have lost its legitimacy. Anti-Nazi deeds were akin to legends in the republic, and represented an important psychological basis for the continuance of quasi-Communist rule. In the past, when destalinization had threatened to topple this pedestal, the regime had responded.[25] In this case, a half-hearted and careless Commission report had left itself open to assaults by those who did not care to divorce the present state from its Stalinist past. Moreover, the criticisms of Barysava-Osipava and Zaharodnik were hardly impregnable. Why would the Germans shoot Soviet citizens with bullets manufactured in 1928, for example? And how does one negate the testimony of fifty-five witnesses who provided information about the NKVD shootings?

In protest at what was perceived to be an official cover-up over Kurapaty, a private initiative called "Committee 58" was created, named after the article of the Soviet criminal code under which the purges were conducted. It was presently renamed "Martyrolog of Belarus" and officially founded in October 1988 under the chairmanship of Paznyak to uncover the crimes carried out under the Stalin regime in Belarus, and to identify those Belarusians who died in this period outside the borders of the republic. It was established at the same meeting that formed the Belarusian Popular Front, hence the process of destalinization, initiated from Moscow, was identified in the Belarusian case with the forces of the opposition.[26]

Kurapaty was a symbol for modern nationhood in that it commemorated those who suffered during the Stalin period. It demonstrated that the Belarusians were as much victims of the regime's malevolence in that period as, for example, the Ukrainians, who were known to have suffered heavily during the purges. Yet it was, essentially, a flawed history; one that remained to be uncovered and explored. Once doubts had been expressed as to the authenticity of the Commission's report, so also was the position of the BPF undermined. Paznyak, its leader, had made the original discoveries, a man denigrated and attacked constantly in the Soviet and post-Soviet press for his unswerving nationalism.

Moreover, Kurapaty elicited strong reactions from those currently outside establishment circles. Within the government and the parliament, the associations with the Soviet period remained too close to begin to delve too deeply into the recent past and former members of the 1930s NKVD were still living in the republic. Thus the official policy appeared to be either to ignore the revelations or else to lay the blame unequivocally upon the German invaders. By 1993 the major historical investigation had come to a standstill, as was noted in a pro-Communist newspaper:

> The bleeding of the cancer on the history of Belarus—Kuropaty—has not healed. Until recently everything seemed to be clear. Thousands of our compatriots were exterminated in the 1930s under the Minsk branch of Stalin's NKVD. However, the other day, the Procurator General of the Republic of Belarus, V. Sholodanov, accepted a decision to reopen the preliminary investigation into the question of the execution of citizens at Kuropaty. Activists of the public commission...have affirmed: the shootings near Minsk were carried out not by employees of the NKVD, but by the Fascists in the Great Patriotic War.[27]

The tragedy remains one of the more startling official cover-ups. One of the leading Belarusian academics in the West has commented that Kurapaty represents the past, and the authorities had no wish to dig it up.[28] He was mistaken. Six years after the end of the Soviet Union, the Belarusian authorities announced suddenly that they were reopening the question in light of "evidence" that the culprits were the Nazi occupants rather than the NKVD.[29] A new version of Kurapaty was about to be written, but promised to be no closer to the truth than the previous inquiries.

BELARUS DECLARES INDEPENDENCE

The year 1990 saw momentous changes in the BSSR. In the spring of this year new elections to the Supreme Soviet were held. Since the Communist Party remained the only legally registered political party, it was able to capture a large majority (around 85%) of the seats. On 23 June, one of its prominent figures, Vyachaslau Kebich, was appointed prime minister. Just over a month later, on 27 July, the Supreme Soviet of Belarus declared state sovereignty.[30] The vote was 230–0, though 120 deputies were absent from the legislature. Belarus laid claim to its own natural resources and its own financial system, including a national bank and state currency. In theory the BSSR was now free to conduct its own foreign relations and declare its neutrality. Finally the declaration stated that the BSSR would support negotiations on a renewed Union of Sovereign Socialist States.[31]

Though this was a significant step forward from the perspective of state development, the occasion was more symbolic than real. It did not signal any dramatic realignment of power. In fact the declaration echoed those of the other former Soviet republics, which had already achieved a breakthrough earlier in the year with the revoking of Article 6 of the Soviet Constitution of 1977, which had guaranteed the Communists a monopoly on power. According to Henadz Hrushavy (Gennadiy Grushevoy), then a member of the opposition BPF, the declaration came as a surprise to most deputies. Further, though the issue had come up earlier, the Communist parliament had rejected it. Two months later, the issue of a declaration was reopened after it had first been approved by Moscow. The BPF was dissatisfied with the notion of reworking the Union which, it maintained, would weaken Belarusian sovereignty by leaving old Union structures in place.[32] That there was a struggle taking place is evident, but initially the contest was one for decision-making between two sets of Communist authorities: one in Moscow; and the other at the regional level.

In March 1991, an All-Union referendum indicated strong support for the continuation of a revised USSR, in the BSSR as elsewhere. Events in Moscow, however, triggered change in Belarus, particularly after Russia declared its independence from the Union in June. After the collapse of the August 1991 putsch in the USSR, the Belarusian republic declared independence on 25 August, five days behind Estonia, four behind Latvia, and one behind Ukraine. The decision was inevitably superficial. Institutions other than the Communist Party (which was soon to be reformed) remained unchanged. The Communist-dominated parliament elected in 1990 remained in place and showed itself prepared to control and even halt the pace of political and economic reform. Initially the CPB was banned, following the ban on the CPSU in Moscow. Then, on 7 December 1991, a new party was formed called the Party of Communists of Belarus. When the old Communist Party was reinstated in February 1993 there were two Communist parties operating in the country.[33] While some of the personalities were different, the

changes at the top can be described as peripheral. Higher level party func-
tionaries were replaced with middle level apparatchiks. The BSSR was
renamed the Republic of Belarus on 19 September, within the same bound-
aries, with the same national capital and thus avoiding the formation of a state
based on any national traditions or cultural heritage. On this same day, the
Supreme Soviet elected Stanislau Shushevich as its chairman (Speaker), a
former Vice-Rector of the Minsk State University. A national flag and symbols were reinstated, namely the white-red-white flag of 1918 and the knight
on horseback coat of arms.

POLITICS IN 1991–1993

The political situation after the declaration of independence did not change
significantly over the next two years. The Republic of Belarus remained
under the control of ex-Communists and reformed Communists. The
Cabinet of Ministers and Supreme Soviet, however, worked more closely
together than in Russia or Ukraine, while the opposition (usually called
"democratic") forces were badly outnumbered, though very vocal. Eighty-
five% of parliamentary deputies were former or current Communist Party
members and appeared to be averse to significant change. The Communists
continued to control most areas of life, including, importantly, the media.
Almost all the daily newspapers had some affiliation with the Cabinet of
Ministers and were completely loyal to its chairman, Vyachaslau Kebich,
whose statements were accorded the same sort of prominence as those of the
General Secretary of the CC CPSU before 1991. In addition, a number of
scurrilous, overtly Stalinist publications began to emerge, the object of which
appeared to be the restoration of the pre-Gorbachev USSR, and which
denounced Shushkevich and other democratic-leaning politicians as "renegades."[34]

Belarus avoided the multiplication of political parties that occurred in
Ukraine where, according to observers there were over seventy registered
parties in the summer of 1993. Nevertheless, there were still more than eleven
registered parties in Belarus, which has a population less than one-fifth that
of Ukraine. Despite the plethora of parties, however, there was a general
uniformity of interests among pro-Communist and conservative factions
within the parliament. They usually supported closer links with Russia, firm
resistance to radical economic reforms, and even (though this was rarely stated
publicly) restoration of the Soviet Union. Given the domination of parliament by these forces, pro-democratic forces could make little impact in the
assembly.

However, the democratic forces in retrospect were quite influential in the period 1991–1993 and to some extent defined the political agenda of the newly independent state. In early 1992, on the initiative of the BPF, a campaign was begun to call a referendum on the question of holding new (democratic) elections to the Supreme Soviet. Over 440,000 signatures were collected, but when the issue was put before the parliament in October 1992 the demand for a referendum was rejected, partly on the grounds that some of the signatures were inadmissible. The BPF saw this and other actions of the legislature as evidence that reactionary forces had gained the ascendant and were trying to roll back some of the important concessions made to the Belarusian national idea during the period of perestroyka. The BPF itself held its Third Convention in May 1993, and decided to form a political component—the Party of the Belarusian Popular Front—in order to contest the next parliamentary election.[35]

The role played by Stanislau Shushkevich is a controversial one and today he is blamed by some democrats in Belarus for the failures of the early post-Soviet period. In December 1991, along with Russian president Boris Yeltsin, and Ukrainian president Leonid Kravchuk, he negotiated the Belavezha settlement at a hunting lodge in Western Belarus, which formally ended the Soviet Union by forming a loose association, referred to in the West as the Commonwealth of Independent States (CIS). By this action, Shushkevich alienated a number of hardline Communists who denounced his action and made him the scapegoat for all future problems. Though formally only the Speaker of parliament, Shushkevich was unquestionably the leading figure in Belarusian politics once he was appointed. According to his own account, the USSR had collapsed well before the leaders met in Belavezha, and the significance of the new accord, in his view, was to have the president of Russia formally acknowledge an independent Belarusian state, an act that was—in Shushkevich's view—unprecedented.[36]

Shushkevich refused to bow to the will of the Communist leadership of the Supreme Soviet and a bitter animosity developed between himself and the prime minister of the republic, Kebich. The rivalry became explosive and ultimately resulted in the removal of Shushkevich on trumped-up corruption charges in January 1994, leaving Kebich the dominant figure in Belarusian politics for the next six months. Kebich was a politician with deep roots in the past. He held a thirty-year membership in the Communist Party prior to the abortive putsch in Moscow in August 1991. Born in 1936 and an engineer by training, he became the Second Party Secretary of the Minsk City Party Committee in 1980, and subsequently headed the section for heavy industry in the CC CPB. In 1984, the zenith of his party career was achieved

with his appointment as Second Secretary of the Minsk Oblast party committee. When appointed the Chairman of the Council of Ministers in 1990, he
was a deputy chairman of the government and chairman of the State Planning Committee of the Belarusian SSR.[37]

Kebich and Shushkevich are the same age, but proved to be quite different
in outlook. Kebich was resistant to fundamental change in the republic. An
intellectual and academic, Shushkevich is the former Pro-Rector of Minsk
State University (with responsibility for scientific affairs) and a short, impa-
tient man, who took on the new position of Chairman of the Supreme Soviet
without a firm power base within the country or in any of the political parties
that had emerged swiftly in the republic. Certainly he was not committed to
any party (though he is a former Communist Party member), and in 1992–
1993 often had serious differences with the Belarusian Popular Front, particularly with Paznyak. The real power in the country lay not with Shushkevich,
but with the Council of Ministers, and gradually the Speaker was placed in
an untenable position that threatened to compromise his principles. The latter were centered on an independent and sovereign Belarus within the Commonwealth of Independent States, and with close economic (but not political
or military) ties with Russia.

Despite his difficult situation, his removal from office in January 1994,
and his eventual demise in the first presidential election of July 1994, each
time any sort of sociological survey was conducted on the popularity of
republican leaders in 1992–1993, Shushkevich was invariably well ahead of
his rivals, Kebich, and the leader of the BPF, Paznyak.[38] One suspects that the
publicity attached to his office of the Speaker was at least partly responsible
for such responses. Most opposition deputies, for example, were not well
known. However, Kebich, operating from his powerful position within the
old party hierarchy, soon attempted to undermine the position of his rival. In
the spring 1993 (Eleventh Extraordinary) session of the parliament, Kebich
advanced what was described as a "strategic initiative" whereby Russia,
Belarus, and Kazakhstan would create a new CIS economic union. He then
tied this to the country's joining a new system of collective security that
linked it with Russia on military questions.[39] The proposal received immediate backing from conservative (pro-Communist) forces inside and outside
the parliament, namely the Belarus faction; the management corpus of
Belarus; and movements sympathetic to the Communists, such as the Union
of Afghan Veterans.[40]

The main arguments offered in favor of the proposal for an economic and
military-political union with Russia were economic ones: that through the
arrangement Belarus would receive better access to raw material and energy

resources at privileged prices, and the numerous enterprises in Belarus directed toward the military industries would receive financing. It was also maintained that collective security was merely a reflection of the times and that all of Europe was moving toward a system of collective security by the year 2000.[41] Among the many commentaries in the Belarusian press in support of collective security was an article by Ihar Hryshan in *Sovetskaya Belorussiya*, on 22 April 1993. He noted that the concept of a Commonwealth or accord had been accepted by Shushkevich, who was cited as declaring that Belarus would be considerably worse off outside the fabric of the CIS. Though the country, Hryshan believed, might have pretensions to "joining Europe," the actuality was the question of tight integration with Russia, Ukraine and Kazakhstan. Neutrality as a status, in his view, could still be pursued within the system of collective security. It would enable good relations with Russia—a prime concern—and could see Belarus adopt a role as a "balancing factor" not only in post-Soviet politics, but by using its central position to enhance the regional array of forces in Europe.

Shushkevich, on the other hand, maintained steadfastly that the CIS collective security system would compromise the neutrality and nonnuclear status of Belarus, and that parliament had no legal right to enter such an agreement.[42] Another observer pointed out other problems, namely that a military union would entail new military expenses for the republic; and that Belarusian youngsters would soon be embroiled in conflicts outside state borders, such as the southern regions of the former USSR. Moreover, he held that the signing of a military agreement with Russia in the past had brought very little solace to the Armenians, whose war with Azerbaidzhan had continued, or to Tadzhikistan, the location of a bitter and protracted civil war.[43] As the debate continued, Shushkevich obtained a proviso that Belarusian soldiers would not be asked to serve outside republican borders. Ultimately, the Kebich proposal was accepted on 9 April 1993 by a majority of parliamentary deputies. It was boycotted by the deputies with affiliation to the BPF, and several individuals abstained on the vote.[44] The interests of Shushkevich and the BPF often seemed to coincide. Though the "alliance" had been purely a working one, interspersed with bitter conflicts, it was effective in undermining some of the positions of the former party leaders. However, the personality rift between the two main figures, Shushkevich and Paznyak, negated most of the opportunities

At this time, Belarus had remained free from the sort of civil strife endemic in many Soviet republics since independence, which forced policy-makers in those states to engage in policy innovations. Whether this passivity was due to a political culture averse to extremism,[45] tardy development of a distinctive national consciousness, and/or lesser resentment of Soviet rule than existed elsewhere,[46] remains uncertain. However, it is clear that the relative tranquility of the Belarus population freed the political elite of irresistible pressures from below for rapid and radical change. Further, the political leadership, Shushkevich excepted, was manifestly averse to economic and political reforms. Dominated by holdovers from the communist regime, this elite sought primarily to consolidate its power and privileges, rather than to wrestle with strategies of breaking out of old structures and orientations. This domination lent a false appearance of stability to Belarusian politics. In reality, the stability was fragile as would become all-too-evident once Belarus elected its first president.

CONCLUSION

The late Gorbachev years and first years of independence were in retrospect a time of democratic progress in Belarus, albeit at a very slow pace. Politically, one of the main distinctions between Belarus and other former Soviet republics, such as Ukraine, was that the opposition and reformists in the Communist Party failed to work together to promote independence. There was general discontentment at receiving directives from Moscow as the center of an empire, particularly with regard to the development of natural resources. But there was no hostility toward closer ties with Russia in general once the empire had been dismantled. The BPF could maintain that in the crucial month of August 1991, the Communists in the Supreme Soviet, in panic after the failure of the putsch in Moscow, had implemented the main provisions of the BPF program: a national independent state that would be nuclear-free and non-aligned. Yet they had done so unwillingly or because there appeared to be no alternative to ensure their survival. In short there was no commitment to independence on the part of those who declared the BSSR to be separated from Russia and the USSR.

This is not to say that there was no political activity in Belarus in support of democratization. In the period 1989–1993 there were numerous street demonstrations in the republic, particularly in Minsk and tied to certain anniversaries such as Chernobyl, or opposed to the price rises on consumer goods that were imposed in the spring of 1991. In the Supreme Soviet, a Democratic Opposition had been formalized by July 1990, comprised of thirty-four deputies, which included the BPF and several independent deputies. It was this group that put pressure on the Communist leaders like Kebich to move Belarus toward independence. As we have shown, though destalinization in the BSSR acquired only a mild form—there was none of the fury that occurred in some republics when revelations from the period of the purges were made public—it nevertheless occurred and raised public consciousness.

What Belarus lacked was a political movement that was not tied to the state administration or to the Communist Party, and at the same time could work with those bodies to promote their aims. Though heavily industrialized, Belarusian society remained in 1990–1993 strangely inert politically. The country was led by an elite, opposed by another elite, while the general masses, conditioned to Soviet rule, were reduced to passive onlookers. During elections they were regarded by some observers as apathetic or disinterested, but it seems that this explanation is simplistic. Rather they perceived their role as distinct from the political process, and it would have been unnatural had they suddenly begun to participate. The statement applies particularly (and perhaps solely) to the older generation which had been cut off from direct participation and public opinion for too long. If they did have enthusiasm for their leadership, then it was confused, obfuscated by images from the Soviet past, from the war (one could not get away from the war in Belarus even in 1989–1993), or from the Masherau era. The smiling, affable Communist-era leader had his name affixed to one of the main streets of Minsk and was recalled fondly on his birthday or the anniversary of his death. It was a peculiarly Belarusian trait, because Soviet-era leaders were not commemorated in Russia (other than Lenin), and Masherau had never been a favorite of the party authorities of the CC CPSU.

Some politicians had grown frustrated with this public attitude, this resistance to change, and general acceptance of the status quo. One politician directed his anger less at the masses than at the government itself, maintaining that if change and reform were to occur in Belarus, they must take place from the top downward. According to Henadz Hrushavy:

> The current government consists of people whose main drawback is their lack of professionalism, but they have a more profound defect. These people formed their experience of state government under the most extreme administrative and bureaucratic system. Thus the potential of the current government is limited by the previous experience of the perestroyka and pre-perestroyka periods. In principle these people cannot act in any other way. They tried to adapt their old ways of ruling the country to the requirements of the present but. . . they are tied to their habits. They apply old methods to new conditions, and become even worse than before.[47]

The economic outlook for Belarus in 1993 appeared grim. Conservative forces believed that citizens were better off under the USSR than in the independent republic. Shushkevich and the democratic forces, on the other hand, had a different, albeit unfulfilled vision. The Speaker of the Supreme Soviet— noting that small European states such as Switzerland have managed to survive and flourish alongside major economic powers—envisaged a non-aligned Belarus as a factor in European politics in the future. From a different perspective, the BPF also foresaw Belarusian integration into Europe some 4–5 years after full privatization and a market economy had been implemented.[48] All these visions were to prove utopian, at least in the short term, though it is fair to say that no political commentators in Belarus predicted the astonishing turn of events of 1994–1997, or that the new democracy would prove to be so short-lived. Nonetheless, the period 1989–1993 ended with Belarus floundering, without a clearly defined policy for economic change, with a static political leadership generally devoid of new ideas, and with an opposition too small to influence decisively the heavily Russified and Sovietized population.

1   See, for example, *Sovetskaya Belorussiya*, 14 July 1989.

2   *Uncaptive Minds*, May–June–July 1989, p. 47.

3   See the compilation of various accounts in *Byelorussian Review*, Vol. 1, No. 3 (1989): 5.

4   Maryla Zielinska, "Bialoruskie Odrodzenie Zianon Pazniak," *Tygodnik Powszechny*, 26 January 1997, p. 5, & ff.

5   Ibid.

6   *Zvyazda*, 14 July 1989.

7   *Shag*, 23 March 1990.

8   At its Third Convention in Minsk, in late May 1993, the BPF decided to form a political party—the Party of the Belarusian Popular Front—to contest the 1994 elections to the parliament. *Zvyazda*, June 1, 1993.

9   Michael Urban and Jan Zaprudnik, "Belarus: A Long Road to Nationhood," in Ian Bremmer and Ray Taras, eds., *Nations and Politics in the Soviet Successor States* (Cambridge: Cambridge University Press, 1993), pp. 109–113.

10 Zyanon Paz'nyak, *Sapraudnae ablichcha* (Minsk, 1992), pp. 48–49. As the leader of the BPF, Paznyak is hardly an impartial source on the subject, but as we will show, even according to official figures, the Belarusian language situation was disastrous.

11 State Administration of Statistics, USSR, *Narodnoe khozyaystvo SSSR 1984* (Moscow: Statistika, 1985), p. 26.

12 V.K. Bandarchik, ed., *Etnicheskie protsessy i obraz zhizni: Na materialakh issledovaniya naseleniya gorodov BSSR* (Minsk, 1980), pp. 203–204.

13 I have discussed this question in David R. Marples, *Belarus: From Soviet Rule to Nuclear Catastrophe*, pp. 21–23.

14 These were hardly dissidents in that they included writers such as V.V. Bykau, holder of the Lenin Prize; and N.N. Arochka, doctor of philology and a senior specialist at the Institute of Literature of the Belarusian Academy of Sciences.

15 *Letters to Gorbachev: New Documents from Soviet Byelorussia* (London: The Association of Byelorussians in Great Britain, 1987).

16 Cited in *Byelorussian Review*, Vol. 2, No. 2 (Summer 1990): 3.

17 "The State Program of Development of the Belarusian language and other national languages in the Belarusian SSR," *Sovetskaya Belorussiya*, 25 September 1990, pp. 1–2.

18 *Litaratura i mastastsva*, 3 June 1988.

19 Ibid.

20 *Sovetskaya Belorussiya*, 22 January 1989.

21 Paznyak's estimates were about ten times this amount. See Urban and Zaprudnik, "Belarus: A Long Road to Statehood," p. 110.

22 The discrepancy here was to lead to problems for the Commission's report. Trees that were as old as 46 years date directly to the period of German occupation, which has provided substantial ammunition for those who have sought to denigrate the Commission's findings.

23 V.P. Korzun, "Menya ne slyshat," *My i vremya*, No. 19 (September 1992): 3.

24 I.Kh. Zagorodnyuk, "Kuropaty: Fal'sifikatsiya veka?" *My i vremya*, No. 19 (September 1992): 2.

25 The regime has long paid homage to the official exploits of the partisans. One of the dominant buildings in Minsk today is the Museum of the Great Patriotic War, which contains four floors of memorabilia and accounts of their exploits.

26 See Art Turevich, "Byelorussia: Genocide of a Nation, Part II" *Byelorussian Review*, Vol. 1, No. 4–5 (Winter 1989–90): 3.

27 *Sovetskaya Belorussiya*, 20 March 1993, p. 3. This is at best, a half-truth. Three Commission members have already produced a major book on the topic (Georgiy Tarnavsky, Valeriy Sobolev and Yevgeny Gorelik, *Kuropaty: sledstviye prodolzhayetsya* [Moscow: Yuridicheskaya literatura, 1990]) and the majority have adhered to the initial conclusion that the NKVD were responsible for the shootings.

28 Dr. Jan Zaprudnik during a panel discussion at the session "Belarus Today," Canadian Association of Slavists annual conference, Carleton University, Ottawa, Canada, 5 June 1993.

29 RFE/RL Daily Report, 24 October 1997.

30 A useful chronology of events can be found in the Appendix to Jan Zaprudnik, *Belarus: At A Crossroads in History*, pp. 229–245.

31 Art Turevich, "Byelorussia's Declaration of Sovereignty: Its Meaning," *Belarusian Review*, Vol. 2, No. 3 (Fall 1990): 2.

32 Grushevoy (Henadz Hrushavy), as cited in ibid., p. 2.

33 *Belinform*, 19 February 1993.

34 One example was the newspaper, *Nash Kompas*, which began publication in January 1993 on a monthly basis. Its masthead featured Marx, Engels, Lenin, and Stalin, and its slogan supported the restoration of socialism under the "banner of Marxism–Leninism Communist-Bolsheviks together with the toiling masses." Its circulation was only 6,000 copies, but it seemed to be carried by most vendors at the old "Union press" outlets. A second was the avowed independent leftist journal *My i vremya*, whose pages regularly contained outrageous cartoons of Boris Yeltsin and other leaders who were considered renegades to the cause of the Communist Party.

35 *Zvyazda*, 1 June 1993.

36 Interview with Stanislau Shushkevich, Supreme Soviet of Belarus, Minsk, 13 October 1996.

37 Roman Yakovlevsky, "Faces and Images," *Minsk Economic News*, No. 4, April 1993, p. 5.

38 For example, on 15 May 1993, the newspaper *Narodnaya hazeta*, published the results of a poll conducted from 722 respondents in the republic, and including all socio-demographic groups of the population. Almost one-third of those polled declared that there was no alternative to Shushkevich as head of state and 53.5% could not state an alternative leader. The remainder opted for Kebich (6.2%), Paznyak (3.7%) and five other leaders ranging in support from 0.4 to 1.6%.

39 According to Art Turevich, the Speaker of the Russian Congress of People's Deputies, Ruslan Khasbulatov, suggested during his 18 March 1993 visit to Minsk, that Russia and Belarus should form a military union limited to those two states. Kebich seemed to prefer a union of three—Russia, Belarus, and Kazakhstan. See *Narodnaya hazeta*, 27 March 1993, p. 1. The original collective security treaty signed in Tashkent on 15 May 1992 included five states: Armenia, Kazakhstan, Kyrgyzstan, Russia, and Uzbekistan. Belarus abstained from signing on the grounds that its official neutrality precluded it from entering into such an arrangement, as did Ukraine and Moldova. See *Narodnaya hazeta*, 7 April 1993, p. 2.

40 Ibid., p. 1.

41 *Sem'dney*, No. 15, 10 April 1993, p. 1. It is argued that in Belarusian military-defense industries in 1992–1993, not a single new type of military product was manufactured.

42 *Zvyazda*, 15 April 1993, p. 1; *Znamya yunosti*, 9 April 1993, p. 1.

43 Sergei Plytkevich, a columnist, in *Narodnaya hazeta*, 17 April 1993, p. 1.

44 *Narodnaya hazeta*, 17 April 1993, p. 2.

45 G. Kuchinsky, "Lord Created Us Centrist," *Minsk Economic News*, No. 3, March 1993.

46 Urban and Zaprudnik, "Belarus: A Long Road to Nationhood," p. 107.

47 Interview with Henadz Hrushavy, Minsk, Belarus, 15 April 1993.

48 *Narodnaya hazeta*, 14 April 1992.

Chapter 4

A NEW PRESIDENCY, JUNE 1994–SPRING 1996

BACKGROUND

The 1994 Constitution specified that Belarus would elect its first president. The election date was established as 23 June 1994. The regulations stated that each candidate must obtain the signatures of seventy parliamentary deputies or 100,000 signatures from the electorate. The signatures were subject to an inspection process from 15 to 27 May, after which candidates could begin their campaigns in earnest. Each candidate was also given the sum of BR20 million for his campaign, and none were permit to solicit or receive contributions from abroad. Stringent rules were also laid out for the election itself: at least 50% of the eligible voters had to go to the polls for the election to be valid, and the winning candidate required more than 50% of the vote to win. If there was no outright winner on the first vote, a run-off would be held two weeks after the declaration of the official results.

Some observers considered that these rules gave an unfair advantage to prime minister Kebich, who had emerged as the dominant figure in Belarusian politics following the dismissal of Shushkevich in January 1994. For one thing, Kebich could easily amass the seventy signatures from parliamentary deputies. By 26 April, nineteen candidates had expressed a desire to run for the presidency, but only a handful of them could be considered serious contenders. Alongside Kebich on the left of the political spectrum there emerged Vasil Novikau, secretary of the Party of Communists of Belarus (PCB), Alyaksandr Dubko, chairman of the Agrarian Union, and Alyaksandr Lukashenka, the head of a government commission on corruption. These candidates could play on the population's fears about the results of privatization and market reform, particularly the concept of "Ukrainization": the view that fundamental economic changes would lead directly to the collapse of the economy (as had ostensibly happened in Ukraine). Ukraine, it was argued, had distanced itself from Russia, and brought about its own economic downfall.[1]

From the democratic standpoint, one of the tragedies of the election was the failure of the various candidates to form a common front. An early candidate was the mayor of Maladzechna, Henadz Karpenka, though he dropped out in the latter stages of the campaign as a result of problems with some of the signatures on his candidacy slip. The BPF leader Zyanon Paznyak, then aged 50, demanded the preservation of an independent and neutral Belarus,

stressing the need to prioritize the Belarusian language and historical heritage. His campaign was marked by the display of the white-red-white flag at
tables on street corners. The main charge levelled against Paznyak, already a
prominent figure in Minsk political life, was what was perceived in some
quarters as "ultranationalism," and a perceived antagonism toward Russia
and Russians. However, his election brochures strongly emphasized the
equality of all citizens of Belarus, regardless of ethnic background.

Stanislau Shushkevich, the effective leader of the country during the later
period of perestroyka and early independence, upset some BPF leaders when
he announced his own candidacy. There had been some serious differences
between Shushkevich and the BPF, and between himself and Paznyak personally, and some Front members argued, with some justice, that he would
succeed only in taking away votes from their candidate on the first ballot.
The BPF felt that Shushkevich had worked too closely with some of the
Communist members of the Supreme Soviet, and that he had proven to be an
unsatisfactory national leader. From Shushkevich's own standpoint, he
could offer himself as a leader who had once been indisputably the most popular politician in the country and one who was not associated with an aver-
sion for things Russian.

The results appeared to surprise almost all observers. After the first round
of voting, Lukashenka was well ahead with 45.1%, followed by Kebich with
17.4%, Paznyak 12.9%, Shushkevich 9.9%, Dubko 6%, and Novikau 4.6%.
The four lagging candidates then dropped out, leaving a final run-off between Lukashenka and Kebich. Suspicions during the first round of voting
that the electorate may have become disillusioned with the political antics of
Kebich were justified by the results of the run-off on 10 July. With a turnout of
around 70%, Lukashenka received 80.1% of votes, or 4.2 out of 5.2 million.
Kebich received 14%.[2] One noteworthy point about this first presidential
election is the relatively strong showing of the two democratic candidates,
Paznyak and Shushkevich, who together had polled almost 23% of the vote,
demonstrating that not all Belarusians had turned against the processes of
market reforms or democratization. By any account, however, Lukashenka
had won an emphatic victory.

Who was the new President? Few people knew much about him. At 39 he
was almost a generation younger than most of the candidates he had defeated.
Tall, receding, and with a prominent moustache, Alyaksandr Hryhoravich
Lukashenka had already proved an effective speaker, with a slightly high-
pitched voice. He was born in the village of Kopys, in the Orsha Raion of
Vitsebsk Oblast on 30 August 1954, and graduated from the Mahileu Teach-
ing Institute and the Belarusian Agricultural Academy. From 1975 to 1977

he was an instructor of political affairs in the Western Border district, and remained in the army for a total of five years. After which he made his career in agriculture, commencing with the position of deputy chairman of the "Udarnik" (Shock-worker) collective farm. For the next eight years he held management and Communist Party posts at collective and state farms, and at a construction materials combine in the Shklau district. In 1987 he was appointed director of the Haradzets State Farm, and used this position to obtain election to the Supreme Soviet of Belarus in the elections of 1990.

In parliament he established a faction called Communists for Democracy. Though there are conflicting accounts of his attitude toward the declaration of independence by Belarus in August 1991, he is said to have been the only deputy in the Supreme Soviet to oppose the Belavezha agreement of December 1991, which brought about (directly or indirectly) the dissolution of the Soviet Union. He maintained close links with hardline Leftist factions in the legislature, including with the Belaya Rus Slavic Congress and the Union of Officers, and it is thought that he had connections with similar groups in Russia, including the Liberal-Democratic Party of Vladimir Zhirinovsky. According to a Western account, Lukashenka's historical heroes were Feliks Dzerzhinsky, the founder of Lenin's secret police, the Cheka; Yuri Andropov, former head of the Soviet KGB and late General Secretary of the Central Committee of the CPSU; and Pyotr Masherau, the former Belarusian party leader.[3] Lukashenka is married with two sons. His wife, who has never lived in Minsk, directs a kindergarten in the Mahileu region, while one of the older sons was studying diplomacy at the Belarusian State University at the time of his father's election as president.

It is difficult even with hindsight to say how much was known about Lukashenka's intentions in the summer of 1994. His career to that point had been markedly low-level and mediocre. There had been little to suggest that he was a future presidential candidate, though the voters were inclined to believe that given his position on the anti-corruption committee, this was a man dedicated to ridding the new republic of criminal and corrupt elements. He was not the choice of the Communist Party, nor did he have much backing in the legislature. Initially he seems to have been content for the most part to fill his Cabinet with some leading figures from the Kebich administration, including Mikhail Myasnikovich, the former deputy prime minister, and Syarhey Linh, formerly the Minister of Economy. As the new prime minister, replacing Kebich, he selected Mikhail Chyhir, a man not known for close links to Kebich or ties to the Communist hierarchy. The new foreign minister, Uladzimir Senka, was a professional diplomat who advocated closer ties with Western Europe. The chairman of the National Bank remained Stanislau Bahdankevich, a man clearly in favor of market reforms.

The BPF and other oppositionists offered the new president what was termed a "100-day grace period." By the end of this time, Lukashenka was already beginning to chastize those around him who questioned his policies. Perhaps the first major evidence of the volatile nature of the new leader was a live TV appearance on 11 November 1994, when he threatened to remove and arrest those who were obstructing his policies, including Chyhir and Bahdankevich. He vowed to take personal control over the KGB, and declared that the recent rises in the prices of food must be stopped. He also attacked state television for broadcasting "unconstructive speeches" and demanded that TV and the press should offer more positive assessments of events.[4] By the end of the year the editors of most of the major newspapers in the country had been replaced. The president had begun to initiate his version of executive rule which showed itself to be singularly sensitive to and intolerant of criticism.

During his public appearances the new president invariably spoke Russian. On one occasion he remarked that he spoke poor Belarusian, but that it could hardly be compared with the two great world languages: English and Russian. One could not express oneself properly in Belarusian, he said. One occasion when Lukashenka spoke Belarusian was during the third anniversary of the declaration of independence on 25 August. For that event he spoke from a prepared text.[5] His Russian was colloquial, filled with phrases to relate him to an audience, using both simple and emotive terms. Though Lukashenka is today regarded as an ardent Russophile, this early period provided no clear manifestation of future policy direction. Lukashenka visited Moscow shortly after his election, but reportedly returned home furious at the coolness of the reception by President Boris Yeltsin, and neither Yeltsin nor his prime minister Viktor Chernomyrdin seemed very interested in developing the concept of a monetary union with Belarus.

THE REFERENDUM OF SPRING 1995

All the post-Soviet states faced the problem of power sharing between the executive and the legislature. The new Constitution of Belarus, issued in 1994, was somewhat vague on this issue, though it had ensured that any president would ultimately be answerable to the parliament. In Russia the contest had ended violently in the Fall of 1993, when Yeltsin turned his tanks on the parliamentary building. Ukraine was slowly reaching an accommodation that would result in an agreement between new president Leonid Kuchma and his legislature in the summer of 1995. For Lukashenka, the issue of limits on presidential powers became the key issue by the spring of 1995 and continued to dominate the politics of his presidency in the months afterward.

There were a number of paradoxes about the contest that developed between the two sides. Parliament was clearly dominated by the forces of the Left, both Communists and former Communists, and Agrarians. Lukashenka appeared to have much in common with these groups and indeed, though he was relatively young for a Soviet-era politician, he came from a similar environment. Like them he deeply regretted the dissolution of the Soviet Union and the loss of political links with Russia. Nonetheless, it would be misleading to regard the parliament as totally alien to reform. The opposition, though small, carried more influence than its numbers might suggest. As in other states, there were also significant divisions among the Communists, some of whom were in favor of market reforms and democratization. It is simplistic to attribute these differences to an urban-rural divide, but there is no question that Lukashenka himself chose his allies from among the rural constituency.

Lukashenka considered the parliament to have run its course. As it had been elected on 25 March 1990, for a five-year period, he maintained that by 25 March 1995 it had ended its mandate. On this question his views were not dissimilar to those of the BPF which had campaigned unsuccessfully for new elections in 1994. The president, however, hinted at going much further, namely dispensing with a parliament altogether. On 14 March he described the legislature as "obstructive" and "dishonest," thus dismissing the body collectively rather than singling out individuals. The deputies, led by chairman Mechyslau Hryb, responded that their mandate had to continue until elections scheduled for 14 May. There could not be a period of interim presidential rule. Hryb already anticipated a future constitutional crisis and noted that the president seemed intent on grabbing power for himself.[6] Three days later, Lukashenka removed the editor of the parliamentary newspaper *Narodnaya hazeta*, Iosif Saredzich, also a parliamentary deputy, after the newspaper published a letter which attacked the president's policies for being too pro-Russian. The newspaper, which enjoyed a very high circulation, had consistently been critical of Lukashenka.

As the parliament's 12th session drew to a close in the second week of April, the president announced his intention to hold a referendum on four highly controversial questions:

1. Do you agree that the Russian language should have an equal status with Belarusian?

2. Do you support the proposal about the establishment of a new state flag and state symbols of the Republic of Belarus?

3. Do you support the actions of the president directed toward economic integration with Russia?

4. Do you agree with the need to introduce changes to the Constitution of Belarus anticipating the pre-term dissolution of the Supreme Soviet by the president of Belarus in cases of systematic or gross violations of the Constitution?[7]

By demanding a referendum on the same day as the parliamentary election, he hoped to prove that his views were closer to those of the electorate than were those of the parliament. He also recognized that with a monopoly over the media and a month to go before the elections he had ample opportunity to make his views known to a public which was already disillusioned with a parliament that had been in power since the Soviet period.

Parliament was divided on how to respond to Lukashenka's demands. Chairman Hryb maintained that there was no juridical alternative but to go ahead with the referendum. Others were more rebellious. On 10 April, Paznyak declared that he and his colleagues would go on a hunger strike to protest the outrageous violation of the 1994 Constitution, and the assault on the Belarusian language and national symbols. Thereafter, fourteen opposition deputies sat on the floor adjacent to the main podium, most of them with newspapers, while in the background the grim figure of Lukashenka glowered from his own elevated podium.[8] Subsequently, the legislature rejected three of the four proposals by Lukashenka, namely those on the status of the Russian language, state flag and national symbols, and the right of the president to dissolve parliament for "constitutional violations." An angry Lukashenka declared that this action would lead him to use force to disband parliament and reschedule the day of the referendum.[9]

This remarkable impasse continued the following day. At 9pm on the following evening (11 April), the hunger strikers were visited by Mikhail Tsesavets, the security chief of government house, and a Mr. Karaleu, the chief officer of the presidential guard, who informed them that they had received information about a bomb being planted in the building. The two visitors demanded that the strikers leave the hall forthwith. This threat appeared an obvious ruse and the deputies declined to be moved. At midnight, a bomb squad arrived and thoroughly searched the premises, finally determining that no bomb could be found. At 3am the parliament was raided by about 200 special force officers, masked and armed with batons, who beat and then forcibly removed the fourteen deputies who were thrown into the back of a truck. According to their own accounts some of the deputies were subsequently subjected to further beatings. Parliament was closed for the morning while police made further searches for the alleged device. Once parliament resumed the session at noon, initially none of the strikers were allowed to return. Though they eventually took their seats, the legislature was suitably cowed and all the president's proposals were meekly accepted.

Thus the first confrontation between Lukashenka and the parliament had resulted in a victory for the president, through the use of force. The precedent of public figures being assaulted by police was an unfortunate one. It had also rendered the referendum more significant than the parliamentary election itself. In the event, all of Lukashenka's proposals were supported by the electorate. The turnout was relatively low at 64.8%. On the status of the Russian language, 83.3% backed the president's proposal; on the question of a new state flag and national symbols, 75.1%; on economic integration with Russia, 83.3%; and on the right of the president to dissolve parliament, 77.7%.[10] Interestingly, these percentages are much less impressive when expressed in terms of the total electorate, at 54%, 48.7%, 54% and 50% respectively. Lukashenka himself did not wait for the results. On 16 May, the national flag was taken down from the president's residence at 38 Karl Marx Street and replaced with the new version, the red-green of the former BSSR, but without the hammer and sickle. It was thus essentially recognizable as the flag used in the republic from 1951 until 19 September 1991.[11]

Why had the electorate apparently rejected the symbols of an emergent nation? The answer lay in both the conditioning of the electorate in the Soviet period and in the effectiveness of the president's propaganda techniques, which successfully portrayed the hunger strikers as extremists. Moreover, most Belarusians in 1995 used Russian as their daily language for both business and at home. Though Belarusian had made significant strides in the period of perestroyka, it had not been widely accepted outside the intelligentsia. National consciousness had yet to embrace a majority of the electorate. Further, the population was unaccustomed to self-initiative or free expression. Just as Shushkevich before him had acquired popularity in part from his position as the leading figure in the country, so too Lukashenka was accepted by many Belarusians simply because he was president. He was also free from aspersions of corruption and appeared to have distanced himself from policies of economic reform that had reduced the living standards of a large portion of the populace. On all these grounds, the public preferred to give the president the benefit of the doubt. He spoke their language. For the opposition, the fruits of several years of activity appeared close to being lost with a single referendum.

THE NEW PARLIAMENT

Though the president had long claimed that the old parliament had outlived its usefulness, he proved to be unwilling to provide much input into the election of a new one. He constantly maligned his main enemy, the BPF, and publicly destroyed his own ballot paper, evidently in an attempt to belittle the importance of the 14 May election. Under the BSSR Supreme Soviet, the rules for the election were similar to those for the presidency a year earlier, requiring a turnout of more than 50% of registered voters and an elected candidate having to receive over 50% of the votes to be elected. This latter rule in particular rendered the filling of seats very difficult. In twenty-four constituencies, the turnout was too low for the votes to be valid. Though elections were validated in 235 constituences (there was one case of the vote being nullified because of electoral violations), only eighteen deputies were elected on 14 May. A second round of elections was held on 28 May, which saw the election of a further 101 deputies, still fifty-four short of the required forum. The elections had not produced a new parliament.[12]

The 1995 elections were the first to be held according to a pluralistic voting procedure. But although a wide variety of political parties and groups participated, few garnered many votes. Of the 119 elected deputies, fifty-three were formally unaligned or independents (many were collective or state farmers), thirty were members of the Agrarian Party and twenty-seven were Communists. The Party of Public Accord obtained three seats, while several parties obtained a single seat each, including the Social Democratic Hramada, the Green Party, the Belarusian Peasants Party, the Belarusian Socialist Party, and the Belarusian Patriotic Movement. Kebich and Hryb were reelected, while Paznyak lost his seat, despite leading the list of candidates on his ballot (he failed to obtain more than 50% of the vote). On 14 June, Lukashenka requested that the old parliament formally hand over its powers to the new. Given the lack of a quorum, however, the old parliament resolved to hold new byelections later in the year and to continue its mandate in the meantime.

The byelections duly took place in late November but once again proved to be indecisive, despite a decision of the old parliament to lower the minimum turnout from 50% to 25%. From 141 contests, twenty deputies were added to the 119 elected in May. A final runoff on 10 December, however, produced a quorate parliament of 198 deputies, twenty-four more than was required by the law, but still leaving sixty-two vacant seats. Of the 198, forty-two were Communists, thirty-three Agrarians, and ninety-six unaffiliated. Though the BPF was no longer a presence in the legislature, several democratic deputies were victorious, including Shushkevich, the former Foreign

Minister Pyotr Krauchanka, and the president of the National Bank of Belarus, Stanislau Bahdankevich. Electoral turnout in the two byelections was better than anticipated at 63% and 52%. Despite official indifference from the president's office, the electorate appeared to have shown confidence in the parliamentary system. Mechyslau Hryb, who had threatened to resign his post as Speaker, had a change of heart and decided to continue in office, thus adding a further major player to the opposition in the anticipated struggle against the intrusions of the president.[13]

FROM DEMOCRACY TO AUTHORITARIANISM

While the protracted efforts to elect a new parliament were taking place, the new president initiated new campaigns in other fields. The years 1988–94 had seen considerable progress in the development of Belarusian culture. In several fields new authoritative works had appeared, particularly in history and literature. In general these works contained the seeds of the de-stalinization campaigns of the late Gorbachev era. In Belarus, this movement necessitated the rewriting of much of the national history. School textbooks were reissued in new editions and contained new interpretations of the Soviet past. The president decided to create a commission to investigate post-Soviet schoolbooks in history and literature, and its conclusion, predictably, was that these new works lacked objectivity and provided a distorted view of events. Presidential spokesperson Uladzimir Zamyatalin noted, for example, that one work of history concluded that Germany and the USSR were equally responsible for the outbreak of the Second World War. Lukashenka promptly prohibited the use of new textbooks and ordered schools once again to use the versions from the Soviet era, a move that some writers regarded as an effort "to turn back the tide of history."[14]

In practice, such a decision proved difficult to implement since many of the Soviet textbooks were no longer available. The president's office had, however, discovered a policy that was likely to assuage some of the public frustration with the problems resulting from perestroyka, which was a straightforward reversion to some of the practices of the Soviet era. It is difficult for the observer, to determine how far such policies genuinely represented the world view of Lukashenka, or how far they were decisions designed to attain for the young president the maximum degree of popularity among what might be termed the old guard and older generation. There had been little indication in his earlier political career of a wholehearted commitment to a reversion to the Soviet era, his vote against the dissolution of the USSR in December 1991 notwithstanding. Nevertheless, by the fall of 1995, the president had begun to adopt policies that would have been acceptable in the era of Masherau.

This statement is borne out by the practical realization of the referendum decision to elevate Russian to the status of a state language. By late August, it was reported on Belarusian Radio, of 25,000 first graders in the city of Minsk, 11,000 would be taught in Russian in the forthcoming 1995–1996 school year, and 5,000 in Belarusian. Parents of the remaining 9,000 children had not yet made up their minds which language would be most preferable for their offspring.[15] Presumably all children would still receive some Belarusian training, but the above example is a firm indicator of the changes that were occurring in language instruction. Any visitor to Minsk in this period could verify the prevalence of the Russian language in virtually all walks of life.

On 12 September 1995, the government found itself transported dramatically back to the Cold War era, when a military helicopter shot down a civilian balloon taking part in an international balloon race. The balloon, which was piloted by two senior Americans Alan Franckel, an airline pilot aged 55; and a 68-year old businessman, John Stuart-Jervis, had strayed accidentally into Belarusian airspace, and reminiscent of the Korean airliner incident of 1983, the helicopter had hovered alongside the balloon for some time before shooting it down on instructions from the anti-aircraft command. Both Americans were killed. Like the Soviet government in 1983, the Belarusians at first refused to accept culpability for the incident. One official remarked that the competition organizers had failed to give sufficient information to the Belarusian authorities about the event. The balloon was reportedly in an area of strategic significance, close to an airfield manned by Russian military personnel. The authorities also noted that two other balloons in the vicinity had landed after being given warnings.[16]

For some time, the Belarusian government clung adamantly to its position. On 2 October, Lukashenka declared that the Belarusian military was not responsible for the tragedy and once again castigated the organizers of the balloon race. Facing mounting anger from the United States, the president changed his mind on the following day, expressing his regret and his condolences to the relatives of the dead pilots.[17] The lengthy delay that had accrued since the incident—almost three full weeks—negated this admission of guilt. Indeed the most notable characteristic of the Lukashenka regime to date was its almost complete lack of concern for international opinion. A less catastrophic but equally astonishing event was to follow, namely a public statement by the president that appeared to praise the Hitler regime.

On 28 November, the president agreed to an interview with the German newspaper *Handelsblatt*, which was subsequently transmitted on Belarusian radio. Lukashenka declared that the history of Belarus was somewhat similar to that of Germany (it should be recalled that Lukashenka graduated in 1975 from the Mahileu Teacher Training Institute with a major in history). Germany had required a strict ruler to raise itself from the ruins of the aftermath of the First World War and the economic problems of the Weimar regime. "And," he added, "not everything connected with Adolf Hitler in Germany was bad...." Germany's quest for an ordered society had continued for centuries and reached its culmination point under Hitler. This was an example for Belarus—and implicitly Belarus under Lukashenka—to follow as a presidential republic. German history teaches that the leading role of the president at this stage in history was critical and indisputable, the president maintained.[18] These statements, which were not clearly thought out, were not only a major public embarrassment for many Belarusians, but they were particularly shocking in the country that had lost about 25% of its population during the years of German occupation.

Throughout 1995 the president's office issued a series of decrees, many of which were declared invalid by the Constitutional Court headed by Valery Tsikhinya. Among the decrees nullified was one on new rules for the byelections. The Court also declared that measures suspending trade unions and invalidating the Soviet-era parliament prior to the attainment of a quorum for the new legislature were unconstitutional. The Court, whose members were appointed directly by parliament, thus acted as a "watchdog" on the actions of the presidency. Consequently, Lukashenka began to seek ways to circumvent such decisions. On 10 November 1995 he declared that he would ignore Court decisions, and he demanded on more than one occasion that Tsikhinya should resign as the Chief Justice. On 1 January 1996, 135 deputies of parliament signed an open letter to the newspaper *Zvyazda*, protesting the harassment of Tsikhinya by the president. The signatories embraced parties across the political spectrum. Indeed, the president had begun to achieve what Shushkevich and Kebich had failed to do: namely to unite the various political groups behind a single overriding cause. In this case, however, the cause was the preservation of the 1994 Constitution.

In late September, a new political grouping emerged called the United Civic Party, consisting of the United Democratic Party, the Civil Party, and the Party for People's Accord, and headed by the reformist deputy, Bahdankevich whose resignation as Chairman of the National Bank of Belarus had been accepted by the president only two weeks earlier.[19] In parliament Bahdankevich, together with Henadz Karpenka, also became the leader of a group called Civic Action in January 1995, formed prior to the opening of the new assembly and dedicated to preserving some of the basic gains of independence: sovereignty and neutrality, a market economy with some social safeguards, and observance of the 1994 Constitution. In the absence of the BPF, the United Civic Party and Civic Action began to emerge as the main opposition party in the legislature, though as yet it was hardly as influential as had been the nationalists.[20] The government would receive its backing only insofar as it adopted a program of reform.

One of the first tasks of the new parliament was to elect a Chair (Speaker) from among its ranks. Lukashenka took a direct interest in this process in the knowledge that the incumbent would likely be the one to contest presidential decrees in the future. He was vehemently opposed to the reelection of Hryb, who eventually decided to remove his name from the ballot (though he still received 18 votes). Of the remaining three candidates, the two leaders were the head of the Agrarian Party, Syamen Sharetski, and the leader of the Communist faction in parliament, Syarhey Kalyakin. In the first round, Sharetski received 51 votes, Kalyakin 50, and Bahdankevich came a respectable third with 38. In the run-off round Sharetski emerged victorious by 108 votes to 88. On paper, Sharetski may have seemed like an amenable choice for the president, as a strong supporter of closer cooperation with Russia and from a party dedicated to rural interests. His appearance was also unthreatening: a fatherly figure with a shock of white hair. Yet conflict between the new Chair and the president began in a matter of days.

Sharetski was 59 when he took office, and a former chairman of a collective farm in the Hrodna region. He had been a founder of the Agrarian Party and its leader since 1992.[21] Under his guidance, the Agrarians had moved away from an alliance with the Communists to a more centralist stance. Sharetski, like his party, was a firm supporter of the Constitution and the preservation of Belarusian sovereignty. He immediately opposed Lukashenka's appointment of one of his close associates, Tamara Vinnikava, as chairperson of the National Bank of Belarus (replacing Bahdankevich) on the grounds that the appointment must be confirmed by the legislature. His parliament was comprised of several caucuses, the largest of which were the Accord (59 deputies) and the Agrarians (47) and the Communists (44). Though the Civic Action caucus under Bahdankevich was relatively small (18 deputies initially) it was bolstered in late February outside the parliament, when the Belarusian Christian Democratic Party joined its alliance of centrist and rightist parties dedicated to market reforms and privatization of land.[22]

Lukashenka meanwhile continued to assert his authority. Once again one of his chief targets (a recurring one) was the media, and particularly opposition newspapers, several of which were now printed in Lithuania, having been denied access to printing facilities in Belarus. On 14 February 1996, the

BPF newspaper *Svaboda* was informed of the cancellation of its lease agreement, effective the following day. The building in which the newspaper was housed was owned by the president's administration. Though the letter breaking the lease claimed that the space was required by the government, the other tenants were allowed to remain. *Svaboda* subsequently moved to a shabby former factory on the outskirts of Minsk. In the following month, the president turned once again on the large circulation parliamentary daily, *Narodnaya hazeta* (published in both the Belarusian and Russian languages), removing its editor Mikola Halko, who had held the job for barely a year, for failure to carry out his obligations. *Narodnaya hazeta* had defied the president by questioning his overtures to Russia (see Chapter 6) and for its concern with the increasing restrictions placed on the media in Belarus.[23]

The restrictions on the press were to continue. On 10 June, the head of the Belarusian State Press Committee announced on television that the operating license of a Minsk business newspaper, *Belaruskaya delovaya gazeta*, had been withdrawn. This newspaper, published in the Russian language, had received five warnings for publishing articles critical of Lukashenka and had been denied the use of printing presses in Belarus (like several others it was being printed in Vilnius). The publishers and the chief editor vowed to continue operations, arguing that the operating license could only be withdrawn through the courts.[24] The government took matters a step further by requesting that all newspapers be reregistered with the authorities. By early July 1996, over 200 newspapers had decided not to go through this process citing financial difficulties. Several newspapers were merged, and a new newspaper, *Belaruskaya presa*, was to be founded for publication abroad to inform an international audience about events in Belarus.[25] As of the fall of 1997, this newspaper had not appeared in the West.

The two high circulation national newspapers in the country remained the former party organ, *Sovetskaya Belorussiya*, and the parliamentary newspaper, *Narodnaya hazeta*. The former had become a mouthpiece of the president, including his photograph on the front page at least once a week and sometimes daily, and promoting his policies, despite the rapid and unpredictable changes of direction. The president has also frequently used the newspaper for the publication of his meandering speeches. Despite the collapse of the Soviet Union, the editorial board declined to change the name of the newspaper. In Kyiv, for example, the corresponding newspaper, *Radyanska Ukraina*,[26] had metamorphosized into *Demokratychna Ukraina*. Though the Minsk newspaper's tone had moderated by the late Gorbachev period, the retention of the name "Soviet" symbolized the reluctance of many circles in

Belarus to embrace fundamental changes during the period of independence. Together with *Vecherniy Minsk*, *Sovetskaya Belorussiya* had become the most pliable popular instrument of the presidential will.

As we have noted, *Narodnaya hazeta* had acted more independently in the early years of independence reflecting the disparate views of the members of parliament. Thus, in the summer of 1996 the president announced his intention to make this newspaper subordinate to the executive branch. The move provoked the anger of Sharetski, who argued that it was a gross violation of the freedom of the press in order to silence critics of the president.[27] The president's move effectively quelled the last official high circulation daily offering criticism of the administration. Henceforth, the public could find objective or alternative analyses only among those newspapers printed outside the country, in *Svaboda*, or in the bimonthly English-language newspaper, *Minsk Economic News*.

The attacks on the media could be defined as petty harassment from a government that was extremely sensitive to criticism. The nature of the regime had evolved from democratic to authoritarian. In the spring of 1996, however, the Lukashenka administration embarked on two new policy directions that appeared to undermine the foundations of the new state. It initiated a new union, or "Community," with Russia (dealt with in Chapter 6) and it resolved to amend the 1994 Constitution by enhancing the power of the presidency vis-a-vis the parliament. The new offensive was heralded by an announcement on 5 March by Lukashenka's chief of staff, Alyaksandr Abramovich, that the president sought constitutional revisions and would if necessary subject them to a national referendum.[28] The revisions would permit the president to dissolve parliament in certain situations, and speculation among the opposition was that they would also pertain to the forthcoming agreement with Russia.

At this stage, the Belarusian Popular Front began to initiate public actions to protest the government's new encroachments on the Constitution. On 24 March, the annual demonstration to commemorate the declaration of independence of 1918 (held a day early to coincide with a weekend) resulted in vicious clashes with the militia. One week later, in advance of the agreement with Russia, the government helped to organize a large demonstration of Communists and trade unionists in support of the event. On the day of the signing, however, about 20,000 people took to the streets of Minsk, again at the behest of the BPF. Two days later, Paznyak travelled to the Ukrainian capital Kiev, in an attempt to rally support for the cause of independent Belarus in the face of what he perceived as forthcoming integration of the republic into Russia. He described the situation as one of internal occupation and a "colonial war by peaceful means." He was in no doubt that loss of independence was imminent. Paznyak also informed his Ukrainian audience that his home was surrounded by militia and that he had been subjected to pressures and harassment.[29]

The climax of this dramatic period of the Lukashenka government came on 26 April, the tenth anniversary of the Chernobyl disaster, and a date when it was known that there would be a sanctioned rally in the streets of Minsk, the first in five years to commemorate this anniversary. The official number of demonstrators was 50,000, though local organizers claimed that at least 80,000 people took part. Following Paznyak's sojourn in Kiev, a Ukrainian fringe group of nationalist extremists, the Ukrainian National Association/Intra-Party Assembly (UNA–UNSO), which had also sent a small number of paramilitary troops to support the cause of the Chechens against Russia, travelled to Minsk for the event. Though the Chernobyl march was not initiated by the BPF, the party ultimately dominated the proceedings. This proved too much for the attentive militia, who initiated a violent clash with the now familiar BPF members. The conflict of 26 April 1996 constituted the first significant civil strife of the post-Soviet era in Belarus, hitherto a state with a reputation for its tranquility and placidity. Scores of people were subjected to charges of militia. A reported 204 people were arrested, including 17 members of UNA–UNSO. Paznyak fled to Moscow shortly after the event, but two of his prominent associates, Yury Khadyka, deputy chairman of the BPF, and Uladzimir Dzyuba, a journalist, were subsequently arrested. Dzyuba's detention was surprising because according to his own account he was not even a participant in the demonstration.[30]

In the aftermath of the events of 26 April, further evidence emerged that the government had begun to adopt repressive measures. The BPF headquarters in Minsk were raided, and an opposition deputy, Pavel Znavets, was detained and held in total isolation for more than twenty-four hours. Parliament protested in vain that it was illegal to arrest a deputy. There were several clear infringements on human and civil rights on the part of the authorities. Anatol Luzin, deaf and dumb from birth, was arrested on charges of shouting "anti-presidential slogans." Over 100 people were put into a prison in the militia headquarters without access either to family members or a lawyer. Even foreigners who had witnessed or participated in the demonstration were rounded up and none were accessible to foreign diplomats for the next thirty days.[31] By 29 April, the authorities announced their intention to prosecute more than 100 of those arrested, some of whom were subsequently jailed for periods up to fifteen days. Several members of the BPF faced more serious charges for their role in organizing the event. Fifteen of those arrested went on hunger strike, including Khadyka and fellow BPF member Vyachaslau Siuchyk.[32]

On the annual May-Day march a week later, a further confrontation occurred when 7,000 demonstrators protesting what they saw as encroachments on national independence converged with a larger protest march of independent trade unionists (sources vary on the numbers involved: from 20,000 to 50,000) close to Independence Square in the center of Minsk. The police attacked the smaller group, in the process assaulting two Russian journalists from the Moscow NTV station who were filming the events. The Lukashenka regime faced criticism from several sides: from the Supreme Soviet for the heavy-handedness of the assault on demonstrators; from the Belarusian Association of Journalists for the persecution of its members; and from the International Helsinki Federation for Human Rights for the continuing incarceration of the two hunger strikers, Khadyka and Siuchyk. Sharetski, on the other hand, blamed the BPF for the escalation of violence. Since 23 March, there had been three major political demonstrations in central Minsk, with more than 200 arrests, and dozens of those arrested left without access to lawyers or relatives.

Two smaller marches were held later in May. On the 14th, about 5,000 people marched through Minsk to demand the release of Khadyka and Siuchyk. The marchers assembled briefly in front of the president's residence but eventually dispersed without incident. A more violent protest occurred on 30 May, involving mainly young people, who carried the former state flag and chanted slogans denouncing the president and in favor of independence. They were led by a youth group called the Party of Freedom and by BPF activists. The militia broke up the demonstrators, who had marched to the president's residence and the central square of Minsk, and arrested 84 people. On this occasion gas and truncheons were used being referred to in official jargon as "special measures." Administrative penalties were imposed on the mainly young offenders of up to fourteen days in prison and/or heavy fines. The parliament resolved to create a special commission to investigate the violent tactics of the police and the OMON troops. Sharetski also spoke out against the persecution of the leaders of the BPF, thus appearing to reverse his earlier comments.[33]

ANALYSIS OF SPRING 1996 EVENTS

What reasons lay behind the confrontations and violence of the spring of 1996? There are several explanations. First, the contest between the government and the BPF, formerly contained for the most part within the legislature, had moved outside the assembly following the BPF's electoral defeat. The BPF had long been depicted by the authorities as a pariah in Belarusian society, as an organization of extremists and fanatics. In reality, it had always faced a fight for survival and had none of the securities of its counterpart organizations in the Baltics and Ukraine, where Popular Fronts and the Rukh could find some common ground with a reformist faction of Communists. Under Lukashenka, the BPF, and particularly its leader Paznyak, were virtually outlawed. The elimination of the BPF from parliament must be attributed, in part, to a sustained and vindictive official campaign and the monopolization of TV and radio stations by the Lukashenka administration to maintain a barrage of propaganda about the BPF.

Reduced to a party on the fringe of political life, the BPF used the occasion of various anniversaries to stage protests: the anniversary of independence, the occasion of the Russia-Belarus agreement, the Chernobyl anniversary, and May-Day. Moreover, Paznyak in particular was constantly in motion soliciting support during the early months of the year, visiting—in addition to Ukraine—Poland and Czechoslovakia. In addition, the BPF appealed to its youth members and sympathizers to take to the streets to protest. The flurry of activity created the impression abroad that Belarus had entered a period of civil strife. In reality, the regime remained secure and there was no real threat to the leadership of Alyaksandr Lukashenka. The most significant feature of these events was that they took place on the streets of central Minsk rather than in the parliament or Constitutional Court. It is likely that this change of tactic of the opposition, albeit forced by circumstances, took the government by surprise. Its initial reaction was heavy-handed and arbitrary.

The events also rendered the legislature somewhat helpless. It was reduced to commentary on the violence and condemnation of the responsible parties, but it was effectively a bystander, whereas in the recent past it had taken an active role in resisting the instrusions of the president. Sharetski was growing increasingly frustrated with the government and referred to the "hotheadedness" of the president, who seemed to wish to control every facet of public life himself.[34]

One of the most effective ploys of the BPF in the spring of 1996 had been to motivate young people to act against the government. The message was not lost on Lukashenka. In mid-June, he addressed an official youth forum and lashed out against teachers of higher educational institutions for conducting "an anti-presidential campaign," and encouraging their students to take part in rallies. In a typical outburst, he described the teachers as "habitual bribe takers" who were opposed to the president for his crackdown on bribe-taking during entrance examinations. A more sinister consequence was that the president ordered students to resist the influence of their professors and teachers and to form an official youth organization, that is one that would support the initiatives of the president.[35]

After two years in office the directions of the new Belarusian government had become clear. It could be termed a revolutionary government seeking retrogressive solutions to Belarusian problems. Lukashenka had begun with a vacillating policy, neither for nor against economic reform, and seemingly uncertain whether to draw closer to Russia or the West. Within six months, the new administration had turned on real and perceived opponents, begun to restrict the activities of the media, and overtly sought increased powers for the executive. In the process, the president had run up against three roadblocks: the Constitution; the Constitutional Court; and the parliament under its new Speaker Sharetski. At the same time, it can be posited that Lukashenka had made the transformation from a rural official to national president without adopting national attitudes or a broader stance on domestic issues. In short, Lukashenka ran the country like his former state farm, cajoling and persuading the peasantry to adopt his policies, alternately issuing threats and expressions of frustration at those who stood in his path. The key crisis was about to develop.

1   David Marples, "Presidential Elections: The View From Miensk," *Belarusian Review*, Vol. 6, No. 1 (Spring 1994): 9, & ff.
2   *Belarusian Review*, Vol. 6, No. 2 (Summer 1994): 5.
3   Ibid.
4   Reuters, 11 November 1994.
5   Reuters, 12 December 1994.
6   Reuters, 16 March 1995.
7   Questions as listed in *Sovetskaya Belorussiya*, 25 May 1997, p. 1.
8   See the photograph in *Sovetskaya Belorussiya*, 12 April 1995, p. 1.
9   The author has described these events in David R. Marples, "Belarus: The Politics of the Presidency," *Belarusian Review*, Vol. 7, No. 2 (Summer 1995): 9. The above and following remarks are based on this essay.
10 *Sovetskaya Belorussiya*, 25 May 1995, p. 1.
11 *Sovetskaya Belorussiya*, 18 May 1995, p. 1.
12 See, for example, Art Turevich, "Elections in Belarus: Their Meaning," *Belarusian Review*, Vol. 7, No. 2 (Summer 1995): 11.
13 David R. Marples, "Belarus: Prospects for 1996," Oxford Analytica Research Brief, December 1996; *Belarusian Review*, Vol. 7, No. 4 (Winter 1995–1996): 7–8.
14 Reuters, 18 August 1995.
15 OMRI Daily Report, 29 August 1995.
16 *Belarusian Review*, Vol. 7, No. 3 (Fall 1995): 1, 24.
17 OMRI Daily Report, 5 October 1995.
18 Reported in *Izvestiya*, 28 November 1995.
19 MMC, 29 September 1995; Belarusian Radio, 18 September 1995.
20 Monitor, 5 January 1996.
21 Ustina Markus, "Siamion Sarecki, New Parliament Speaker," *Belarusian Review*, Vol. 8, No. 1 (Spring 1996): 2–3.
22 OMRI Daily Reports, 19 January 1996; 28 February 1996.

23 OMRI Daily Reports, 23 February 1996; 20 March 1996.

24 Monitor, 10 June 1996.

25 OMRI Daily Report, 9 July 1996.

26 The correct form of the name is *Radyans'ka Ukraina* (Soviet Ukraine). I have omitted soft signs from text transliterations for the purposes of simplicity.

27 Interfax, 8 July 1996.

28 Monitor, 5 March 1996.

29 Intelnews, 4 April 1996.

30 David R. Marples, "More Demonstrations and Arrests in Belarus," Oxford Analytica Research brief, May 1996.

31 *Svaboda*, 11 March 1997, p. 3.

32 Marples, "More Demonstrations and Arrests in Belarus," & ff.

33 Monitor, 31 May 1996, and 3 June 1996; Reuters, Interfax, NTV (Moscow), 30 May 1996.

34 See, for example, OMRI Daily Report, 5 June 1996.

35 Interfax, Monitor, 17–19 June 1996.

Chapter 5

LUKASHENKA'S CONSOLIDATION OF POWER

By the summer of 1996, President Lukashenka began to consolidate his authority as president through constitutional means. Since the first post-independence Constitution did not permit such an extension of executive power, the administration planned to make amendments to it and have them approved by a referendum.

In July 1996 the president outlined his plan for an amended version of the 1994 Constitution. It encompassed two chambers: the House of Represent-atives and the Council of the Republic. The House of Representatives was to have 110 deputies, elected by secret ballot. The Council was to be an assem-bly of territorial representation. Each oblast and the city of Minsk were to elect deputies through secret ballot at meetings of local Soviets, making a total of eight. A further eight were to be selected by the president himself. There was an age differential between the two chambers: the House could comprise any citizen of Belarus over the age of 21, whereas to sit in the Council of the Republic, a representative had to be at least 30 years of age. No deputy could be a member of both chambers simultaneously.[1]

Lukashenka demanded the right to dissolve parliament if it failed to approve the president's choice of prime minister twice. Parliament would also lose the right to veto senior appointments, such as defense, interior and political ministers.[2] The president would decide on election dates, the times of parliamentary sessions, would appoint judges, the officials of the Central Electoral Commission and half the members of the Constitutional Court (hitherto all nine members of the Court had been selected by the legislature). He also wished to extend the term of office of the president from five to seven years, and suggested some restrictions on private landownership.[3] All the above demands could be resolved by means of a referendum on the anni-versary of the October Revolution, 7 November 1996. This announcement constituted a blatant power grab and was perceived as such by both the major political parties and the Constitutional Court.

On 24 July, seven parties from across the political spectrum issued a joint statement accusing the president of trying to establish a dictatorship. The president had consistently violated the Constitution—by definition Lukashenka had committed this transgression since his whole purpose was to change drastically the nature of the Constitution adopted in 1994—and had chosen to ignore the rulings of the Constitutional Court. He was also accused of the mismanagement of economic policy and leading the country into international isolation. The call for yet another referendum was seen as a ploy to avoid parliamentary opposition to the latest round of measures to enhance presidential authority. Deputy Speaker Henadz Karpenka referred to the new program as an "anti-constitutional coup" and urged a five-year moratorium on any changes to the Constitution.[4] Sharetski issued a statement declaring his intention to oppose Lukashenka's plan to alter the Constitution without securing a mandate from parliament.[5]

Three days later, about 15,000 demonstrators marched to commemorate the sixth anniversary of the declaration of sovereignty in 1990.[6] Some 10,000 armed troops watched the procession, in which demonstrators carried the national white-red-white flag. The occasion saw the commencement of a campaign, initiated by parties of the center and right—the United Civic Party, the Social Democratic Hramada, and the Belarusian Popular Front were included—to collect signatures from parliamentary deputies to impeach the president. According to Article 104 of the 1994 Constitution, an impeachment process required the support of at least two-thirds of parliamentary deputies, but the issue could be raised with the support of only seventy deputies.[7] Did impeachment have a chance of success? The answer is that it was the last resort of deputies confounded by the latest threat of the executive to bypass their authority. It was an effective counter-move, particularly since the president could not be certain of the outcome of a vote in the house, though the ultimate result was unlikely to favor the parliamentarians.

At the end of July 1996, word reached Belarus that the BPF leader, Zyanon Paznyak, together with BPF spokesperson, Syarhey Navumchyk, had applied for asylum in the United States. Both stated that they feared for their lives if they returned to their homeland because the president had said they would be "neutralized." This news prompted an angry outburst from the president who declared that the two were "terminally ill cases." He predicted that the opposition leaders would soon be resorting to violence to get their way, and would "break through apartment windows and rape your wives and daughters." At different times in the period 29 July to 5 August, the president declared that he would place a ban on all rallies during the harvest season and would not tolerate any attempts to remove him from office. He would, he declared, seek to remain president for two more terms—a statement that prompted the derogatory appellation among the opposition of "Alyaksandr Lukashenka, president for life." In addition, the national holiday would be changed from 27 July (the day of the declaration of sovereignty) to 3 July (the day when the city of Minsk was liberated from German occupation in 1944).[8]

In mid-August the president visited Hrodna, on the Polish border, in a pre-referendum campaign. He informed onlookers that further byelections to the parliament on 24 November were unnecessary because parliament already had sufficient members. On 31 August the new draft constitution was presented by the president to the public. Perhaps the most flagrant abuse of democratic rights was the revelation that the new version of the Constitution would be debated on 14 September by a body termed the First Belarusian National Congress, composed of 6,000 delegates from all regions, all handpicked by the presidential administration. Early in September, sixty parliamentary deputies also met with Lukashenka and signed a statement in support of the proposed referendum and the presidents' demands.

The juxtaposition of forces in the fall of 1996 was confusing. On paper, the parliamentary opposition led by the Speaker Sharetski appeared to have a clear majority in the legislature. On 5 September, for example, when an opponent of the president, Viktar Hanchar, was elected chairman of the Central Election Commission, giving him overall responsibility for the by-elections and presidential referendum, he received 111 votes, with only 43 opposed out of 199 delegates. Communist support for the opposition was unreliable, however, and Lukashenka was effective in putting pressure on deputies in the rural areas in his former home region. On 2 September, an alliance of fourteen political parties and movements held a mass rally in central Minsk. Parliament was openly supported by the chairman of the Constitutional Court, Valery Tsikhinya, and his deputy, Valery Fadzeyau, who stated that the draft constitution presented by Lukashenka was anti-democratic and scarcely imaginable in a state located in the center of Europe.[9]

Lukashenka had begun to sound increasingly truculent, at least to a foreign ear. On 26 September, he referred to the lawmakers as: "These nationalist radicals, these fascistic swindlers who have stolen the name of represent-atives of the new Belarus…the voting at the referendum is a vote of confidence in the president."[10] In the same month, the bank accounts of the remaining press organs critical of the administration were frozen, and they received heavy fines for alleged tax violations. The measure encompassed the following newspapers: *Belaruskaya gazeta*, *Belaruskaya delovaya gazeta*, *Belaruskiy rynok*, and *Imya*. At the same time, the president also dismissed his new defense minister Leanid Maltseu, in what appeared to be a staged operation, with Maltseu consuming alcohol at a gathering and then being fired on grounds of personal misconduct for being intoxicated when delivering a speech to the Minsk Medical Institute.[11]

On 11 October, with the overt support of Chairman of the Constitutional Court Tsikhinya, the Supreme Soviet voted 88–84 in support of a referendum on the possible abolition of the post of president. At the same time, Lukashenka had secured the signatures of 110 deputies for his own proposal. Once again parliament appeared evenly split and irresolute on the issue of division of powers. On 19 October, the president made his first conciliatory gesture, agreeing to postpone his referendum until 24 November, so that the electorate could choose between his ideas and those of the legislature. Both Tsikhinya and Sharetski were using the term "dictatorship" with reference to the likely consequences of a presidential victory. The confrontation was created almost entirely by the government, with parliament lacking initiative and being obliged to respond to the latest overture from the office of the president.

Though Lukashenka had a team of advisers, and his relentless spokesperson Zamyatalin, the clash with parliament and oppositionists generally, was very much the result of a personal campaign by the president. The campaign was subtle in that Lukashenka chose to discredit the parliament on a number of occasions by denying its credibility in the eyes of the people. As we have noted, there was no dominant political group in the legislature. In fact when the deputies did reach a consensus, it was invariably in response to the latest outrageous statement or gesture from Lukashenka. Sharetski had taken on the role of parliamentary leader, but he seemed strangely unsuited for the task: quiet spoken, placid, and easygoing in front of the TV camera, his personality was in marked contrast to the angry and emotional president. As the crisis moved toward its culmination point, Sharetski seemed increasingly unsure of his position.

Lukashenka made his appeal directly to the public, thereby denying that parliament was a truly representative body. There was logic to the approach. The first Constitution had been debated extensively in parliament among lawmakers, but it had not been presented to the public. It was not a bad Constitution, the president acknowledged in a published statement, but there could never be peace and agreement in the country as long as it remained in force. Rather, there was constant disagreement and debate (he omitted from the text, naturally enough, that he was the chief source of the disagreement and debate). The conception of the abolition of the president, his message implied, would lead to a swift return to the era of "privatization," a time when the interests of the public would be ignored. There had already been a time of lawlessness and disorder under Shushkevich, when the people suffered various deprivations. The new Constitution would benefit not the president, nor the parliament, but the people of Belarus. Above this address was a large photograph of a smiling Lukashenka surrounded by legions of cheering supporters.[12]

To the domestic audience, the president had identified the opposition with the recent past (the era of perestroyka), remembered as a time of suffering. It was relatively easy to equate market reforms with poverty and corruption. Clearly many people would consider such a statement accurate. In a personal interview during the buildup to the referendum, in October 1996, Henadz Hrushavy noted that reforms in the former Soviet Union had to be initiated by the leadership. Because of the nature of the former Soviet system, they could not be a grassroots phenomenon because the public had yet to learn the concept of self-help. In Russia, Boris Yeltsin had turned on the former Soviet leaders and led the country toward reforms; whereas in Belarus, Lukashenka had chastized the first *post*-Soviet leaders, and thus turned against the path of reform. One could add to this an addendum, namely that despite a military assault on the parliament, Yeltsin's opponents were eventually amnestied. Lukashenka showed no indication of agreeing to any form of compromise or any restrictions on his authority.

THE NOVEMBER CRISIS

November 1996 will be remembered as the month of crisis in Belarus, the most dramatic period in the republic since the Second World War. It is arguable, however, that the crisis was artificial, created by the executive in order for amendments to be made to the Constitution. The view of the Constitutional Court was that the president's changes amounted to a new Constitution. Sharetski declared that if the changes were accepted, Belarus would become a "fascist-like" dictatorship. Lukashenka himself cited the example of France under Charles De Gaulle as a model (a more fortunate example than Adolf Hitler's Germany), maintaining that during times of crisis countries required a strong, executive government.[13] De Gaulle, however, had not resorted to such abusive language about the legislature, nor had he victimized the media. By the start of November 1996, when both sides wished to make their views known to the electorate, the media had been effectively silenced.

There was one significant exception, namely the Russian television stations broadcasting from Minsk, which had already provoked the anger of the president by their frankness in reporting. On 13 November, Minsk correspondents for the Russian ORT and NTV stations were threatened with expulsion from the country if they continued broadcasts critical of the presidency. Four days later, Lukashenka publicly warned that he would halt

Russian broadcasts into Belarus. The issue was more significant than it may have appeared to some observers. The majority of Belarusians had access only to three television stations. Belarusian TV, on the first channel, had been reduced to a mouthpiece of the presidency. In November 1996, not only did the president make regular personal appearances—often for several hours at a time—but even round-table discussions on the referendum, of which there were many, were notable for declining to hear the side of the opposition. Indeed Sharetski himself had been banned from making TV appearances.[14] The other two stations were both Moscow-based.

In the run-up to the referendum, presidential slogans adorned streets, busses, and subway trains. The one posted most often declared simply: "Referendum—The Future Is In Your Hands!" The period between 14 and 20 November saw an escalation of the conflict, to the extent that there was open talk in Minsk about the outbreak of a civil war. Such rumors exaggerated the situation because the opposition simply lacked the means to oppose the executive, which had long courted the military and the police, and frequently resorted to violence to achieve its ends. Nevertheless, the situation soon became very serious, beginning on 14 November, when Viktar Hanchar, a former ally of the president who had become a bitter opponent of his regime, was abruptly dismissed as the Chairman of the Electoral Commission.

Hanchar had declared that he could not affix his signature to the results of the referendum because they were contrary to electoral law. On the following day, the militia surrounded the offices in which Hanchar and his colleagues worked, and forcibly evicted them from the parliament, a move that prompted parliamentary deputies to spend the next night in the building in case the tactic was repeated. On 16 and 17 November, protesters took to the streets in Independence Square. On the latter date they were attacked by armed militia, and many were beaten and injured, including several parliamentary deputies. On 18 November, the prime minister, Mikhail Chyhir, tendered his resignation. He was promptly replaced by Syarhey Linh as acting prime minister (the appointment was later made permanent).[15] On this same date, parliamentary deputies began to circulate a petition calling for the removal of the president. A minimum of seventy-three signatures was required to get the process under way.

In retrospect, this campaign was somewhat naive, because the deputies lacked the firm support required to remove the president. Over two-thirds of deputies in a full parliament (260 seats) would have been required, or 174 votes. Of the 199 members currently sitting, Lukashenka had at least 60 committed supporters and others who were reluctant to oppose him overtly. Impeachment and removal were thus not realistic possibilities. On 19

November, however, the Constitution Court also began inquiries into the president's infringements of the Constitution. The judges had some support from outside the republic. The presidents of Poland, Ukraine, and Lithuania also voiced their support for the preservation of organs that upheld the independence and democracy of Belarus. Their initiative received backing from Europe and North America, though Russia was conspicuous by its silence.[16] Russia was, however, concerned, having vital interests at stake in Belarus.

THE RUSSIAN INTERVENTION

On 20 November, Russian president Boris Yeltsin spoke to Lukashenka by telephone, and the following day, Russian prime minister Viktor Chernomyrdin arrived in Minsk, accompanied by Yegor Stroyev, Chairman of the Federation Council, and Gennadiy Serlechnikov, Speaker of the Russian Duma. The Russian intervention may have been related to the 2 April Community agreement, which rendered Russian interest in the internal politics of its neighbor legitimate. The arrival of the Russian delegation did suggest, however, that the Belarusians were incapable of healing their internal squabbles. From Lukashenka's perspective, he could hardly refuse Russian mediation having championed the Russian cause since the summer of 1994. Yet he had more to lose than did parliament's representative, Speaker Sharetski. On the other hand, some deputies and oppositionists did not believe that Sharetski should have negotiated at all. When he did so, Belarusian sovereignty was called into question.

On the night of 21 November, Chernomyrdin, Lukashenka, and Sharetski talked for ten hours. The Russian side was evidently determined to come up with a compromise solution, and in the morning the three parties duly signed an agreement. The president promised that the results of the referendum would not be binding, and parliament agreed to withhold its complaints about Lukashenka from being heard in the Constitutional Court. After twenty days, the parties agreed, a Constituent Assembly would be formed that would draft a new Constitution. The Assembly would have 100 delegates: half to be chosen by the president; and half by the parliament. However, the chairman of this Assembly would be Lukashenka. The Constitution would be elaborated based on the results of the 24 November plebiscite.[17] Having reached this remarkable compromise, the Russian delegation returned to Moscow, leaving behind general dissatisfaction.

There was little chance that parliament would ratify the compromise agreement with a two-thirds majority. Many deputies regarded Sharetski's role as treacherous, since he appeared to have conceded the right of the president to call the referendum. The Speaker thus had acknowledged a process that had no grounding whatsoever in the existing Constitution. Further, since parliament could not muster the necessary numbers to support the compromise solution, Lukashenka promptly revoked his one concession, namely that the results of the referendum would not be binding. In fact the entire compromise gave much legitimacy to Lukashenka's position, crowned with the notion that he would chair a new assembly. As one observer noted, "Because of the union between the two countries, Russia had the right to intercede, but this gave the semblance of pseudo-legal camouflage to actions that were overtly illegal."[18]

In practice, the plebiscite was already in progress, harnessed by the presidential machinery. The Moscow interlude was a facade that served to strengthen the position of the president while committing him to very little. In addition it effectively ended the role of Sharetski as the standard bearer of the legislature. Whether that had been one of Lukashenka's goals from the outset is a moot point. The only debatable point is how Lukashenka would have reacted if parliament had, for some reason, chosen to accept the Russian compromise.

THE REFERENDUM

The voting process for the referendum began at least two weeks ahead of the 24 November dateline. Voting cards were mailed to some of the electorate, to be filled out and returned. Many village residents voted several times. Factory workers reportedly received threats that their wages would be withheld if they refused to support the president's demands on the referendum. On the day of the referendum, vodka and beer were provided at polling stations in an effort to entice people to vote, and the process was supervised by the president's personal staff. Ballot boxes were carried through the villages as in tsarist times to encourage people to vote. In university dormitories, it was noted in a non-Belarusian source, lists of those students who had declined to vote were posted, and these students would face the consequences, such as being expelled or suspended from university.[19]

The night before the referendum, the president appeared on Belarusian television to inform voters that they faced a simple choice: order or chaos. No Soviet election had provided more partisan propaganda than the campaign of November 1996. Outside Belarus (and possibly Russia) few observers regarded the procedures as either legitimate or democratic. What puzzled some observers was the alleged idiosyncratic voting habits of the electorate, as 24% of the electorate reportedly turned out to vote during the last four hours of the referendum. Two observers from Ukraine discovered a package of unmarked ballot papers at one of the polling stations in the city of Brest, and they were subsequently arrested.[20]

Altogether, over 84% of the electorate took part in a referendum on seven questions, including those inserted by the parliament. They were as follows:

1. Should the national holiday of Belarus be changed from 27 July to 3 July, when Belarus was liberated from Nazi Germany?
2. Do you support the new Constitution offered by the president, which would extend his term in office from five to seven years; permit him to appoint half the members of the Constitutional Court and the electoral commission, in addition to a new upper house of sixty senators, while the number of seats in the parliament would be reduced to 110?
3. Do you support the unrestricted buying and selling of land? [A negative response was implied—DRM]
4. Should the death penalty be abolished? [A negative response was implied—DRM]
5. Do you support the draft referendum offered by the parliamentary deputies that would abolish the office of president and invest authority in the cabinet headed by a prime minister?
6. Do you support the election of regional leaders [appointed by the president]?
7. Do you approve of funding for state institutions directly from the budget?

The first phrase of the second clause above requires a brief explanation. In theory, Lukashenka was not asking for a longer period for a presidential term. It remained five years, renewable for a second term. He had, however, already been in office for twenty-eight months by the time of the referendum, and wished to then "restart" his term once the revisions to the Constitution had been confirmed, meaning that his mandate now runs until November 2001, at which time he can seek a second term that would take him through to November 2006, or slightly less than 12.5 years in total.

A reported 70.5% of voters supported the new draft constitution of the president, who was successful on all his issues, receiving the most support for the question on the national holiday (88.5%). A large majority rejected the abolition of the death penalty and elections of heads of local administrations. The official tally followed some very misleading reports in the immediate aftermath of the referendum. At some voting stations, the initial count was that 100% (and sometimes more!) had participated in voting. At the second count, the total dropped to 90%, before reaching the official figure of 84% noted above. The newspaper *Imya* provided a cynical comment on the proceedings that now the president could appoint his own man to the position of Senator, and could dismiss parliament and the government at any time.[21]

The results of the referendum constituted a resounding victory for the president. One should acknowledge that the president's popularity in some quarters was genuine. He had targeted several groups for the bulk of his propaganda: the rural constituents; the elderly; the military; and the KGB. While the aforementioned groups made up a minority of the population, they constituted a majority of the voters on 24 November. It has been noted, for example, that the highest voter turnout was in the Homel region (a Russophone, former Communist heartland), and the highest individual totals were among the KGB and the military, with an official tally of 99.6%.[22] On the other hand, the lowest turnout was in the city of Minsk, the location in which the forces of the opposition were at their strongest. Thus whatever the irregularities of the process—and there were many—it would be misleading to dismiss the popularity of the president as a figment of his imagination. He provided a strong leadership figure reminiscent of the Soviet era.

After the referendum, the president appointed 110 members of the current parliament to the lower chamber of a new body called the House of Representatives. The new upper house or Council of the Republic was also established. The international community ignored invitations to attend a ceremony marking the introduction of the new, revised Constitution.[23] Members of the parliament not selected to the new House were permitted only to retrieve their personal effects. In addition the 24 November election results were simply ignored. Candidates elected to office were not permitted to enter the 110-seat assembly. The president also had the authority to dissolve either house at any time, and had additional powers to replace members of both the Constitutional Court and Economic Court.[24] A presidential power grab had thus been completed through a quasi-legal framework. The process was blatantly undemocratic, but the forces against the president quickly collapsed.

The proposed impeachment was abandoned once it became clear that twelve out of the seventy-three deputies who had begun the process had had a change of heart.[25] Some deputies tried to assemble in the House of Writers, including the former Speaker Sharetski (now replaced by Anatol Malafeyeu [Malofeev] in the new legislature). Their efforts were relatively futile. Belarus was criticized abroad for the high-handed actions of its president, particularly at an OSCE meeting in Lisbon. The European Union also urged Lukashenka to adhere to democratic principles. (The Russian Duma, on the other hand, recognized the new assembly.) There was little hope of such admonishments and advice being received positively in Minsk. Lukashenka had taken just thirty months to consolidate his authority and create a presidential republic. Thereafter, the opposition, or indeed even neutrals, simply had no outlet for their grievances. Belarus was never isolated, because it could always turn to Russia. Whether or not Russia had sought greater control over its neighbor was a debatable point (see Chapter 6).

By late December, an amended Constitution had been consigned to press, and it appeared in a bilingual edition, with a circulation of 200,000 copies, early in 1997. To provide a facade of respectability, it was described simply as the Constitution of the Republic of Belarus of 1994 with the addendum (with changes and amendments) added after the title. The implication was given that as a result of a plebiscite, several changes had been made, but essentially the Constitution of 1994 was intact. In reality, Belarus had a new Constitution which gave exceptional powers to the president. The changes are exemplified by the state of the Constitutional Court, formerly selected by the parliament. Under the amended Constitution, six members of the Court are to be chosen by the Council of the Republic and six by the president, and the president also has the main responsibility for the selection of the Chairman of the Court (Article 116). Since the president also can appoint half the members of the Council of the Republic, then there is no possibility in the future of his encountering the sort of problems presented by a recalcitrant judge such as Valery Tsikhinya.

On the other hand, the dictatorship was not yet complete. The contraction of the legislature in some ways benefitted parties like the Belarusian Popular Front, which had been obliged for several months to operate outside the parliament. Though Paznyak was abroad, the BPF was far from inactive.[26] In addition, though the political opposition had been considerably weakened, and the government had established complete control over the official media, there were several other public organizations in Belarus which operated outside the government domain. Ostensibly there was no political threat to the regime from these groups. But in the partisan perspective of the government, any organization that operated freely outside its purview should be targeted: first by being obliged to reregister with the authorities; second by having taxes and charges raised on its property; and third, by being subjected to a government inspection and audit.

NEW PRESIDENTIAL OFFENSIVES, SPRING 1997

Two major political changes occurred prior to the renewed presidential campaign to augment his powers. In December, after a meeting with

Lukashenka, Vasil Kapitan, the country's prosecutor general, resigned. Kapitan was regarded as one of the last remaining powerful independent figures. He was promptly replaced by Aleh Bazhelka, a close political associate of the president. In the following month came the more startling news that another close political ally, Tamara Vinnikava, who had been appointed chairperson of the National Bank only after a prolonged struggle with parliament, had been arrested for alleged financial misdoings at her previous job with Belarusbank. Not only was Vinnikava arrested, but she was incarcerated for two months without trial, after which the authorities declared she would serve a further three months.[27] In October 1997 she remained in prison in the main KGB headquarters in Minsk, where she was reportedly ailing. This vindictiveness toward one of Lukashenka's former close associates served as a warning to other presidential employees that their positions were subject to the whims of the president.

In March 1997, the government targeted public organizations for inspection and harassment. The extent of the assault was revealed in a Declaration of the Belarusian Rights Protection Committee, comprising 130 public organizations, published on 12 May 1997. The Declaration noted that "presidentially controlled organs" had put acute pressure on the largest independent organizations in the areas of humanitarian aid (the Children of Chernobyl Fund), cultural-enlightenment activities (The Society of Belarusian Language), and science (The National Center of Strategic Initiatives "East-West"), all organizations that were well known both inside the country and abroad. The leaders of these organizations had been discredited in the media. The independent press had been denied typographical facilities. Finally the Belarusian Soros Foundation had been targeted for special treatment with a financial penalty of $3 million.[28]

Two of the main victims, as noted, were the Belarusian Soros Foundation (BSF) and the Belarusian Charitable Fund "For the Children of Chernobyl." In the recent past, the president had toyed with the idea of taxing the Soros Foundation, despite the fact that the organization had spent a reported $10 million to assist the country in 1995–96. On 16 March, the head of the BSF, Peter Byrne, was detained for eighteen hours at the Minsk-2 International Airport when trying to reenter the country, before being deported to Germany on the grounds that he had taken part in illegal meetings of the opposition. The accusations were strongly denied by Byrne. Subsequently the bank account of the BSF was seized, and it was obliged to suspend its activities in Belarus.[29] On 15 May, George Soros wrote a letter to President Lukashenka protesting the illegal seizure of the bank account, and maintaining that the attempt to close the BSF was "politically motivated and lacks a basis in law."[30]

The "Children of Chernobyl" Fund was under investigation by a special commission of the KGB for several weeks in the spring of 1997. Despite three previous audits of its accounts, the new investigation of its books resulted in two major accusations: that it had indulged in political activities on behalf of the opposition—a realistic charge in that the Fund had been started under the auspices of the BPF, though it became independent shortly thereafter; and that Iryna Hrushavaya, a Fund board member and wife of the Fund's president, Henadz Hrushavy, had been involved in financial improprieties when children were sent from Belarus to Germany in 1991 (an old KGB charge based on the rates of exchange between the mark and the ruble that had not been verified by the previous audits). In typical fashion, the charge against Iryna Hrushavaya was announced on national television on 23 April. Both Hrushavy and his wife were in Germany at this time. Henadz Hrushavy, nonetheless, returned to Belarus briefly to lead the "Chernobyl Way" march through central Minsk on 26 April.[31]

On 6 April, a major Western charitable organization, Citihope International, issued a press release which announced that it had suspended its care giving programs in Belarus, including those that had offered aid to children suffering from the Chernobyl disaster. Citihope had maintained a presence in Belarus for seven years under its president, Reverend Paul Moore. However, its international arm, the Nadezhda Express, had been subjected to unwarranted taxation, as had food supplies brought into the country. Citihope had provided over $130 million worth of aid to Belarus, including medicine, medical supplies, food and clothing, including a final cargo worth $4.6 million that arrived in Minsk on 5 April. What had led to this situation? From March 1996 to April 1997, eight inspections had been conducted of Nadezhda Express by organs such as the Ministry of Finance and the Department of the Presidential Administration, and some BR6 billion taken in the form of taxes from the charitable organization. Appeals directly to the president had been to no avail.[32]

The vindictiveness of the government was vividly evident in the turbulent spring of 1997, the traditional time for marches and demonstrations commemorating a number of anniversaries. The first public rally occurred on 23 March, for the anniversary of independence. It was brutally dispersed by government troops. Among those detained was the co-leader of the Civic Action bloc in the former parliament, Henadz Karpenka, and several foreigners, some of whom were merely observing events. One was Serge Alexandrov, the First Secretary of the US Embassy in Minsk. Alexandrov, whose ancestry is Belarusian, was declared "persona non grata" and given twenty-four hours to leave the country. The United States responded by expelling the First Secretary of the Embassy of Belarus in Washington, Uladzimir Hramyka. The newly appointed Belarusian ambassador to the United States, Valery Tsepkalo, was informed that he would not be welcome in the country "for some time," and US Ambassador Kenneth Yalowitz was recalled to Washington for discussions.[33] The United States was clearly outraged by the harassment of its diplomatic personnel in the center of Minsk.

On 2 April, as Belarus and Russia were signing a formal Union agreement (see Chapter 6), a large protest took place, which again was subject to the intervention of the militia. The clash was the most violent to date. Over 100 arrests were made. Descriptions of incidents abound. Among the most poignant was the depiction of Valery Shchukin, a correspondent of the newspaper *Tovarishch*, lying on the ground and being beaten by militia. At a press conference later, he remarked on the paradox that he, a Communist, was being attacked on Kommunisticheskaya Street. The scenes of brutality were seen by many Belarusian viewers on Russian Television. Lukashenka declared that such scenes had been fabricated. On 26 March, the government introduced stricter rules for the foreign media. Foreign news agencies were prohibited from entering the government's satellite communications center without prior accreditation from the Foreign Ministry. All news materials had first to be presented to the officer on duty for censorship.[34]

On 25 March, an employee of Russian NTV, Aleksandr Stupnikov, a citizen of Israel living in Belarus with a Belarusian wife, was informed that he no longer had accreditation in the country, and the following day, the deputy chairman of the presidential administration, Ivan Pashkevich, stated that Stupnikov must leave the country by the end of March. The Russian government expressed concern at such treatment of its employees—other journalists received warnings—but the Belarusian response was that the majority of people concerned were Belarusian citizens, thus the matter was an internal one. Stupnikov's case was significant in that it was the first deportation of a journalist from the country, and moreover one with firm roots in Belarus.[35] The measures did not bring a halt to public protests. On 9 April, 5,000 workers took to the streets to demand payment of wage arrears.[36]

As opposition to the regime was manifested in the public rallies, the government began to search for scapegoats. In early April, the president appeared on television accusing the Polish minority of the Hrodna region of plotting against him. He would not, he asserted, permit another Yugoslavia situation to emerge in Western Belarus. Sources concur that there was no evidence of any ethnic tension in Hrodna region, where even the two major churches, Orthodox and Roman Catholic, cooperated in charity work. However, some 3,000 Poles had participated in an opposition demonstration.[37] On 18 April, a bomb exploded in a Minsk apartment, prompting government allegations that a new terrorist wing had been formed within the BPF. Allegedly a note had been found after the bomb went off promising further actions against OMON troops if there were any problems at the forthcoming Chernobyl March on 26 April.[38] The note was written in English, and can be regarded as a crude provocation on the part of the government. The BPF had never resorted to the use of terrorism in the past.

Though the 26 April march was the first peaceful demonstration of the season, the events since the referendum had left the country in turmoil. The president had not yet succeeded in establishing a full dictatorship—such rallies could hardly have taken place had he done so—but he had applied extreme force against his alleged enemies. Indeed, the president's authority was extended to all facets of life. Even prominent citizens and former leaders, such as Shushkevich, were subjected to detainment and harassment. The ex-Speaker of the parliament Mechyslau Hryb was fined $1,000, for example, for organizing a rally to commemorate the first post-Soviet Constitution. Society was subjected to new rules, inspections, arbitrary arrests, and even attempted assassinations of known oppositionists. Even foreigners and diplomats were no longer immune from government encroachment. In a period of less than a year, Belarus had been transformed politically into a repressive state that infringed grossly on the most basic human rights. Underlying the crackdown was the revised—in reality, new—Constitution, which provided legal justification for the greatly enhanced powers of the president.

These powers were formally ratified on 24 June by the upper house of the parliament, without discussion and in the absence of the president, illustrating the extent of Lukashenka's authority over this body. The president was now able to appoint his own prime minister and deputy ministers, and the Chairperson of the National Bank; he had authority to dissolve both houses of parliament, to convoke parliamentary elections in "exceptional" circumstances, or to hold referenda, all by the simple issue of a presidential decree.[39] The president's consolidation of power marked the complete reversal of a move initiated by the former parliament in 1995 to define and to restrict the authority of the president. By the summer of 1997, Belarus was ruled as a presidential dictatorship, though there were still several loopholes that prevented the regime from wielding all-pervasive powers—not least its general inefficiency.

The crucial question is why these events occurred in a republic known for its general passivity, if not apathy, toward matters political. The answer lies in the personality of the president. Lukashenka is very much a rural apparatchik with a narrow but clear vision of the society he wishes to create. It is trite to declare simply that this is a conception of a Sovietized society, or a reversion to the past. No leader based in Minsk has ever wielded such authority. On the other hand, the measures also suggest a fundamental insecurity as much as a lust for power. Enemies loom very large in the world view of Alyaksandr Lukashenka. Without such enemies, it would be difficult to justify the new authority of the president, admittedly, but there are reasons to suggest that the insecurity is genuine. The president has been ridiculed for his lack of culture, poor knowledge of the native language, and general boorishness. He has been seen to be unusually sensitive to ridicule and sarcasm, such as that exhibited by the newspaper *Svaboda*, among others.

In March 1997, the Belarusian Popular Front issued a statement that the events of that month led its members to question seriously the president's mental competence. The people had become hostages to his "personality, desires, moods, and possible medical conditions." The president, however, was acting in a manner contrary to the sort of behavior accepted in the civilized world. The raids on the opposition, arbitrary detention, persecution of the press, and deportation of foreign citizens were cited. He had offered complimentary comments about Adolf Hitler and he was "irrationally obsessed" with the idea of union with Russia. Since Lukashenka commanded a powerful army, what was needed, the BPF declared, was an objective evaluation of his mental health.[40] While such a comment may illuminate only the dark side of Lukashenka's personality, it nonetheless raises the issue of whether the president was acting in a rational manner. Most outside observers, examining the events of 1996–97, would have responded in the negative.

The president in this period was rarely calm. His public appearances were daily and characterized by impatience, irritation, and outright fury against his opponents. Initially he used the powers assigned to his office to get his way. Ultimately he acquired new authority so that by the summer of 1997, his powers were close to complete. It should be noted, however, that politics was but one sphere of his domain. In another, the president's position was less certain, namely Belarus' relationship with the outside world, and in particular, Russia, a country with which he had declared affinity but which in the economic sphere had advanced much further than Belarus on the path of economic reform. This relationship cannot be separated entirely from domestic repressions which, by the spring and summer of 1997, had extended to Minsk employees of the Russian television station ORT. It is to these issues that we now turn.

1   *Kanstytutsyya Respubliki Belarus' 1994 goda (sa zmyanennyami i dapaunennyami). Prynyata na respublikanskim referendume 24 listapada 1996 goda* (Minsk: Belarus, 1997), pp. 27–28.

2   On 4 May 1996, parliament had approved several appointments after some initial resistance: Leanid Maltseu as the minister of defense; Uladzimir Matskevich as the head of state security; and Tamara Vinnikava as the chairperson of the National Bank of Belarus.

3   *Nezavisimaya gazeta*, 23 July 1996.

4   Interfax, Reuters, 24 July 1996; OMRI Daily Report, 18 July 1996.

5   Interfax, 22 July 1996.

6   In Belarus, this date—27 July 1990—was celebrated rather than the official anniversary of the declaration of independence, 24 August 1991.

7   OMRI Daily Report, 29 July 1996.

8   Reuters, 29 July 1996; Reuters, 5 August 1996; OMRI Daily Report, 31 July 1996.

9   Belapan, Interfax, 31 August to 5 September 1996.

10 Moscow, MTK Television, 26 September 1996.

11 Belapan, Interfax, Monitor, 4–6 September 1996; *Minsk Economic News*, No. 21, November 1996, p. 1.

12 Aleksandr Lukashenko, "Tol'ko narod vprave vybirat' svoyu sud'bu!," *Sovetskaya Belorussiya*, special issue, November 1996, p. 1.

13 Wlodzimierz Poc, "Slonina Wyborcza," *Wprost*, 24 November 1996, p. 87.

14 Ibid.

15 Jagienka Wilczak, "Bialoruskie Demony," *Politika*, 30 November 1996, p. 15.

16 Mikhail Pastukhov, "Impichment ne sostoyalsya. A moglo li byt' inache?" *Narodnaya volya*, 2 March 1997, p. 3.

17 OMRI Daily Report, 22 November 1996.

18 Andrzej Romanowski, "Bialorus: test dla Rosji," *Tygodnik Powszechny*, 1 December 1996, p. 3.

19 Maria Graczyk, Wlodzimierz Pac, "Fajny Car." *Wprost*, 1 December 1996, p. 94.

20 Yuri Drakokhrust, "Referendum: New Era Begins," *Minsk Economic News*, No. 23, December 1996, p. 2.

21 Cited in Graczyk and Pac, "Fajny Car."

22 The figure is cited by Ustina Markus in the OMRI Daily Report of 26 November 1996. It is doubtful that such a figure is authentic, though there is no reason to doubt the enthusiasm of the KGB and the military for the strongarm tactics of the president. The military, in particular, had suffered as much as any sector of society during the period of perestroyka.

23 The draft plan was published on 9 November 1996 in a special issued of the newspaper *Sovetskaya Belorussiya*, with a circulation of four million copies. It gave the president extensive and sweeping powers. For example, with the token consent of the upper house (Council of the Republic), over which he already had control, the president could appoint six members of the Central Electoral Commission; the Prime Minister; the Chairpersons of the Constitutional Court, Supreme Soviet, and Supreme Economic Court; the Chairperson of the Central Electoral Commission and the National Bank of Belarus.

24 *Minsk Economic News*, No. 23, December 1996, p. 6.

25 OMRI Daily Report, 27 November 1996.

26 In an interview published in December 1996, Paznyak declared that "The opposition, the Popular Front, plans to pursue a constant battle with the regime. They are going to organize rallies, demonstrations, pickets, and protests, despite the fact that many of the ministers have decided to side with the junta." Pawel Bawolec, "Reka Moskwy," *Wprost*, 15 December 1996, p. 83.

27 *Minsk Economic News*, No. 6, March 1997, p. 5.

28 *Belaruskaya maladzyezhnaya*, 16 May 1997, p. 17.

29 David R. Marples, "Belarus: The New Dictatorship of Eastern Europe?" *Belarusian Review*, Vol. 9, No. 1 (Spring 1997).

30 Open Society Institute, 15 May 1997.

31 For details of the charges against the Fund, see *Imya*, 29 April 1997, p. 17.

32 Cited in *Belarusian Review*, Vol. 9, No. 2 (Summer 1997): 17.

33 Marples, "Belarus: The New Dictatorship of Eastern Europe?"

34 *Minsk Economic News*, No. 7, April 1997, p. 1.

35 Ibid.

36 *Svaboda*, 11 April 1997, p. 1.

37 Piotr Gabryel and Maria Graczyk, "Front Wewnetrzny," *Wprost*, 6 April 1997, p. 90.

38 *Izvestiya*, 18 April 1997, p. 2.

39 "Belarus Between Dialogue and Polarization," *The Jamestown Foundation Prism*, Vol. III, No. 10, Part 1, 27 June 1997.

40 Published inter alia in *Minsk Economic News*, No. 7, April 1997, p. 1.

Chapter 6

RELATIONS WITH RUSSIA

INTRODUCTION

Relations with Russia have always been critical for Belarus. The legacy of the Soviet period has been much debated, but there is no question that Belarusians have diverse feelings toward and images of their giant neighbor. The declaration of independence and the 1994 Constitution had stated that Belarus was to be a neutral, nonaligned state. Russia, however, had annexed Belarusian territories in the Soviet period, particularly in the 1930s. After the Second World War, the official policy of Russification had an impact on all facets of cultural life and consciousness. In the Shushkevich era, one of the stumbling blocks for the Speaker vis-a-vis his political enemies had been the proposal by prime minister Kebich to enter a military and security union with Russia. Arguably this issue was one of the factors behind the downfall of Shushkevich who could not reconcile himself to the loss of sovereignty that such an agreement implied.

Alyaksandr Lukashenka's election campaign indicated that he would draw the country closer to Russia. In itself, the manifestos meant little. In Ukraine, for example, Leonid Kuchma had been elected on a similar platform, but once in office had continued the process of nation building, distancing himself from Russia, and particularly Russian influence in policy making. Though Russia was considered Belarus' closest friend, in Lukashenka's view, there is reason to doubt that he considered Boris Yeltsin as the best candidate for the Russian presidency. One of the paradoxes of Lukashenka's presidency is that it came to power denouncing the Belavezha agreement of 1991 that founded the Commonwealth of Independent States, but then was obliged to deal directly and personally with one of the signatories to that agreement—if not its actual architect—Boris Yeltsin. One could detect during the Russian election campaign of 1996 and subsequently that Lukashenka would have preferred to deal with Aleksandr Lebed or even Communist leader Gennadiy Zyuganov than with Boris Yeltsin, the ailing but reform-minded leader.

BELARUS IN THE INTERNATIONAL ARENA

Prior to the electoral victory of Lukashenka, Belarus had taken several measures in the sphere of nuclear nonproliferation. The dissolution of the Soviet Union left the new state as one of four former Soviet republics to possess nuclear weapons, both tactical and strategic, in addition to being the site of several military bases and a rocket facility near the town of Lida (Hrodna Oblast). Along with the newly formed Belarusian army of approximately 80,000 troops, Belarus entered the new era as one of the most militarized countries in Europe. One in every eleven citizens was a member of the military. The new country hastened to demonstrate to the world that its intentions were peaceful. In May 1992, for example, it signed, along with Russia, Ukraine, and Kazakhstan (the other nuclear arms holders) a protocol to the Strategic Arms Reduction Treaty with the United States. In this same year, the Shushkevich government declined to sign the Tashkent agreement of the CIS countries on the grounds that the treaty would violate Belarusian neutrality.

This portent of Belarus' intentions was followed up in February 1993 when the Belarusian parliament ratified the START-1 Treaty and voted also to accept the Nonproliferation Treaty as a neutral country, as outlined subsequently in the 1994 Constitution. In January 1995, Belarusian Foreign Minister, Uladzimir Sianko, was in Brussels to sign an agreement joining the NATO Partnership for Peace Program. There had been some concern in Minsk whether adherence to the Treaty was not in contravention of the neutral stance required by the Constitution.[1]

In October 1992, Belarus had also been a signatory to the Conventional Armed Forces in Europe (CFE) Treaty, by which it agreed to decrease and restrict in the future tanks, combat aircraft, and other weaponry.[2] In late October 1995, an American delegation visited Minsk, led by the US Secretary of State's special advisor on CIS affairs, James Collins, and the US Defense Secretary's advisor on international security, Ashton Carter. The two sides announced that in 1996, Russian strategic rocket troops would also be leaving Belarusian territory, following the removal of nuclear weapons.[3] In June 1996, the US raised the sum provided to Belarus under the Nunn-Lugar Program to $28.9 million, which was to be used for dismantling weapons and rocket fuel without damaging the natural environment.[4]

By early 1996, Belarus had begun to comply with the provisions of the CFE Treaty, and by late November 1996, all nuclear weapons had been removed from Belarusian territory to Russia for dismantling. Lukashenka was inconsistent on the question of nuclear weapons in Belarus, particularly when faced with the prospect of NATO expansion into Poland and Hungary. In June 1995, he had announced that he would suspend the transfer of weapons to Russia, which he claimed was a mistaken policy devised under the previous leadership.[5] In January 1996, speaking to academicians in Moscow, he threatened to redeploy the weapons in response to NATO's "provocations."

At this time, only eighteen SS-25 missiles remained in Belarus, but the president hinted that they could be used as a bargaining ploy with the United States and that some compensation could be demanded.[6] These comments can be written off as presidential blustering. The removal of weapons continued. On 26 November, an official ceremony was held at a railroad station twenty miles south of Lida to mark the transfer to Russia of the last SS-25 missile on Belarusian territory. The ceremony was attended by Acting Minister of Defense, Alyaksandr Chumakou and Russian Minister of Defense, Igor Rodionov.[7]

These measures were initiated during the early post-Soviet period, when relations between the United States and Russia were extremely cordial. In this same period, Belarus was designated the capital of the CIS, a situation that must have irritated the new president beyond measure. The CIS, however, though it developed as a military alliance, could never succeed as long as major players remained reluctant to participate in it. Ukraine in particular remained aloof and from a strategic perspective, Ukraine was particularly important for Russia, being not only a border region, but also the location of the Black Sea Fleet. Under such circumstances, it appeared to be more expedient for Russia to pursue its strategic objectives through bilateral treaties; what were termed in Moscow "treaties of friendship and cooperation." By late 1994, with the Russian army inside Chechnya, the close relationship with the United States began to cool. The latter country, in turn, began to develop more friendly relations with Ukraine, increasingly considered a more reliable partner.

Belarus was not a major player in these events, but its continuing friendship became important to Russia given the apparent vacillations of the Ukrainians toward signing a major treaty with Russia (ultimately signed, though not ratified by the respective parliaments, only in May 1997). Reliable partners were few and far between, thus despite the political repressions carried out under the Lukashenka administration, Russia could scarcely abandon its ally or even administer a serious warning for its undemocratic behavior. (Such an admonishment would also have been hypocritical given the way in which the Yeltsin regime had resolved its own conflict with a parliamentary opposition.)

What sort of friendship did Belarusians want with Russia? Opinion polls conducted in this period suggest that many would have gone beyond mere partnership. According to one comprehensive survey, 55% of Belarusian residents wanted to see the restoration of the Soviet Union or some sort of Slavic Union, in which Belarus would be more closely integrated with Russia. An even higher proportion—63%—preferred a simple union with Russia.

Some 45% also expressed a preference for a socialist system.[8] Was this a death wish? In an era of heightened nationalist tension in places like the former Yugoslavia and even Canada (over Quebec), the majority of Belarusians appeared to wish to reject statehood, to give up the experiment as impossible and return to the Russian fold. This mindset also included the new president, Alyaksandr Lukashenka, though with the provision that in the process he would not relinquish his own authority. Ultimately those two goals were to prove irreconcilable and mutually exclusive.

RUSSIA–BELARUS: FIRST STEPS

The program begun under prime minister Kebich to develop closer relations with Russia reached its fruition with a treaty of 12 April 1994, on a monetary union between the two states. There were three basic provisions to this treaty. First, starting 1 May 1994, there would be no further customs restrictions between the two countries, and the price of Russian oil entering Belarus would accordingly fall by $40 per ton. Second, effective July or August 1994, there was to be agreement on a fixed rate of exchange between the Belarusian rubel (*zaichyk*)[9] and its Russian counterpart, within the range of BR5–7 to the Russian ruble. Finally, Russia was to offer credit to Belarus to meet its balance of payments, commencing with the equivalent of approximately $115 million in the first half of 1994 (see also Chapter 2).[10] The agreement appeared to benefit Belarus far more than Russia, and it was evident that some hard bargaining would be required once a new president took office in Minsk.

For Lukashenka, Russophile that he was, the result was a near catastrophe. His August 1994 summit with Boris Yeltsin was highly unsatisfactory, as the Russians made numerous demands on Belarus, particularly Russian prime minister Viktor Chernomyrdin. What had appeared as a triumphal first summit in the aftermath of a remarkable election victory became almost a public humiliation for the first president of Belarus. On 10 September, Chernomyrdin revealed the extent of the differences between the two sides when he remarked that there would be no monetary union with Belarus because economically, Russia was much further advanced economically and thus such an arrangement would hardly be expedient. He noted that salaries in Russia were ten times higher than in Belarus. There was no practical advantage to Russia in adhering to such a union with a poverty stricken partner.[11] Lukashenka shortly afterward met with Ukrainian president Leonid Kuchma and announced his intention to meet also with the presidents of Poland and Lithuania (Lech Walesa and Algirdas Brazauskas), implying that he would if necessary seek new partners.

Given his political outlook, however, Lukashenka was fundamentally uni-directional. Though an economic union was not feasible, it was possible to explore the limits of cooperation with Russia. In early January 1995, the two sides decided to form a customs union and signed a series of agreements as a prelude to such an arrangement. The customs union would provide Russian oil and gas at below market prices and would save Belarus about $400 mil-lion a year once it came into force in the spring. The agreement also encom-passed Russian military bases on Belarusian territory, and Belarus agreed to the maintenance of such outposts—in particular an anti-missile station in Baranavichi and a radio station in Vileyka—for a 25-year period.[12] The cus-toms union agreement marked a breakthrough for the Belarusian government and defined a future policy which would be oriented ever closer to Russia.

A major symbolic event was the signing on 21 February 1995 of a Treaty of Friendship and Cooperation between the two presidents. Boris Yeltsin arrived in Minsk and in a speech to the Belarusian Academy of Sciences declared that Russia and Belarus were especially close partners. There might be, he suggested, a development of a two-tier system within the CIS, in which Russia, Belarus, and Kazakhstan would be more closely integrated than the other partners. The two sides revealed that there would be joint customs re-gulations and joint protection of the border regions. The BPF leader Zyanon Paznyak denounced the treaty as the first step in the incorporation of Belarus into Russia. Yeltsin, who also visited the MAZ truck factory in Minsk, assured onlookers that history could not be turned back and there was no thought of restoring the Soviet Union. However, the two sides had reached no agreement on prices for oil exported to Belarus (the Belarusian debt was constantly mounting).[13]

Belarusian frustrations with the lack of progress on gas and oil prices surfaced in late 1995. Prime Minister Mikhail Chyhir and Deputy Prime Minister Syarhey Linh both declared that Belarus was facing increased prices. The culprit, in their view, was Gazprom, the giant complex that ran the Russian gas industry and appeared to be acting independently of the Russian government. Gazprom had not only raised prices, it had requested the imme-diate payment of interest on Belarusian debts. Nor would Gazprom accept payment in kind—compensation for the continuing maintenance of Russian military bases in Belarus, for example. Chyhir was particularly concerned that Belarus had also received nothing in return for the parts of nuclear weapons shipped to Russia.[14] The country had made the required sacrifices, but in neither case had the Russian side responded.

On the anniversary of the Treaty of Friendship and Cooperation, Lukash-enka travelled to Moscow, ostensibly to define the nature of the customs union and what form of integration the two countries might take. In February 1996, President Yeltsin was facing a difficult situation. Diagnosed as having a serious heart condition and with stiff competition in the election campaign for a second term as president (the election was in June 1996), he was acutely conscious of the popularity of integration with former Soviet states as an election issue. The discussions of February 1996 were wide-ranging and sometimes contradictory. Economic cooperation would be increased, but in Yeltsin's view integration would be the first step, union a possible (but by implication not a likely) future scenario. About $470 million in state credits owed to Russia by Belarus would be cancelled. The prospect emerged of a broad customs union embracing Russia, Belarus, Kazakhstan, and Kyrgyzstan. The Russian side also announced its intention to approach Poland regarding a road link between Belarus and the isolated Russian enclave of Kaliningrad Oblast, though the Poles were noncommittal.[15]

How far the two governments were prepared to go in the process of integration was revealed on 2 April 1996, when the they founded an organization entitled the Community of Sovereign Republics (CSR) in Moscow. The name itself suggested that integration was already in progress, and in some respects the CSR was reminiscent of Mikhail Gorbachev's plans for a restored Soviet Union in the spring and summer of 1991. The two presidents appeared together in Red Square and informed the expectant throng that their respective states had joined in political and economic integration, but that each country would retain its sovereignty. The countries would preserve their independence, state flags and national symbols but they would combine their policies in several significant areas, including foreign policy, economic reforms, transport, energy, and in the development of a single currency by the end of 1997. The two sides would draw up a common budget, create a single customs system, and combine laws on taxation and investment.[16]

The Treaty created three new organs: a Supreme Council as the major organization, to be composed of the highest officials of each state, with Lukashenka appointed as Chair for the first two-year period; an Executive Committee, to be headed by Russian prime minister Chernomyrdin; and a Parliamentary Assembly. In practice, the Executive Committee would be the most active working group. A joint budget would be elaborated by Lukashenka's associate Mikhail Myasnikovich and Russian Vice-Premier Aleksey Bolshakov. The treaty would go into effect in August and thereafter 2 April would be for Belarusians a day of popular unity and a public holiday.[17] Lukashenka had fulfilled his election promise and the CSR received widespread publicity in Belarus. The Russian interpretation was more circumspect. *Pravda*, for example, declared that the "Union" was no more than a form of expression. The two countries had not formed a union along the lines of 1922, it added, but rather closer integration and cooperation in certain spheres.[18]

In short, Russia may have perceived the CSR differently from Belarus. For Boris Yeltsin, it was a useful reelection ploy but it is difficult to discern how far he was committed to the concept of a new community with one of the weakest potential economic partners in the CIS. The concept was well received in Russia and received praise from Aleksey II, Patriarch of Moscow, in a statement delivered over Easter.[19] (Lukashenka had already declared the Orthodox Church to be the official religion of Belarus and was working closely with Filaret, the leader of that church in the country.) Within Belarus, the CSR was broadly accepted. According to an opinion poll cited by the Open Media Research Institute in Prague, a poll of 300 people indicated that 47% of respondents were fully in support of the agreement, while 16% supported it in part, and 16% were opposed. The impact of the CSR on Belarusian sovereignty received mixed response: 30% felt that it would consolidate sovereignty, 28% that sovereignty would be lost, and 16% thought the impact would be minimal.[20]

The Belarusian parliament also ratified the treaty by 166 votes to 3, and the Russian State Duma approved it unanimously. To the BPF, however, the CSR was anathema, an indicator that Belarus was not interested in preserving its independence. The 2 April saw extensive protests in the city of Minsk, and on the following day BPF leader Paznyak travelled to Kyiv to publicize the situation in Belarus to residents of Ukraine. Clearly, Belarus had moved closer to Russia. The appearance of Russian customs officials on the Polish border of Belarus was an illustration of how far matters had developed. On the other hand, there were limits thus far to the integration. Of significance was that the government had demonstrated its intention to develop its initiatives, foreign policy directions, and economic policies exclusively toward Russia. It is these factors rather than potential loss of sovereignty that mark the importance of the CSR. There is no evidence that the authority of the Belarusian president was significantly reduced or, for that matter, that he would pay attention to Russian views on how he conducted domestic affairs in Belarus. Conversely, the Belarusian impact on Russian policy making remained negligible. The CSR may have enhanced—as it surely did—Russian influence in Belarus. It had no impact on Belarusian influence in Russia, other than to serve notice that Belarus would remain a close friend in all situations.

Some limitations on the CSR were clarified in June 1996, when the Russia–Belarus Parliamentary Assembly met in Smolensk and rejected the concept of a single Russian-Belarusian citizenship. One of the principal opponents was Sharetski, the Speaker of the Belarusian parliament, who felt that the idea would nullify Belarusian statehood. Instead citizens of each country were to be permitted equal opportunities for employment, housing, and social benefits in the other state.[21] Sharetski was designated the chair of the Parliamentary Assembly for a two-year period and a number of commissions were created to work on the various issues, all to be housed in Moscow. The two presidents met once again on 22 June in Minsk and resolved to merge customs services. The customs arrangement soon ran into difficulties because of Belarus' state-imposed protectionist policy. A visit by Bolshakov to Minsk in late July resolved little.[22] The economic policies of the two countries remained fundamentally different.

As Russia and Belarus struggled to resolve these issues, the Chairman of the Security Committee of the Russian Duma, Viktor Ilyukhin, made an astonishing statement that caused as much embarrassment to the Russian government as to the Belarusian. Ilyukhin maintained that he had come across information that the CIA had created a task force of eighteen officers in Warsaw that intended to overthrow the Lukashenka government, separate Belarus from Russia, and bring it into the Western orbit. The information allegedly specified that Solidarity-type unions would be created in major Belarusian cities to organize strikes and demonstrations, using the aid of Ukrainian nationalists. It was even stated that one or two BPF leaders would be assassinated and their deaths blamed on Lukashenka, after which the president would be impeached by parliament.[23] Few observers gave much credence to these remarks, though they were exploited by the Belarusian government to heighten the impression of "outside enemies" working against Belarus and its foreign policy directions.

The Belarusian side consistently maintained that integration with Russia was of benefit to both sides, and that Russia had vital interests in Belarus that would be protected by the 2 April Treaty. Russian pipelines to Europe, for example, passed through Belarusian territory, and the military bases constituted another important factor. Belarus also provided links to the Kaliningrad region—the subject had begun to crop up frequently in Belarusian propaganda. In December, Belarus received some support for its perspective from the Russian Minister for CIS Affairs, Aman Tuleyev, who acknowledged that of all the countries of the former Soviet Union, only Belarus offered a genuine prospect of integration with Russia.[24] How far this statement reflected official thinking in Moscow is debatable. In April 1997, however, the two countries intended to go much further than the CSR, and mark the anniversary with an actual Union.

THE UNION TREATY

The Treaty of 2 April 1997 has been regarded widely as a virtual renunciation of independence by Belarus. It transformed the Community into a
Union. The Treaty and Charter of the Union were accompanied by a Memorandum of mutual understanding pertaining to the "amendment and adoption of the Charter of the Belarus-Russia Union." The Treaty was clouded by
differences between the two sides which could barely be concealed by the
toadying official press of Belarus and propaganda emanating from the president's office. The original version of the Treaty, drawn up by the Belarusian
side, ran to some eighteen pages before it was sent to Moscow for revisions
from the Russian leadership. It was returned in a reduced three-page version,
which committed Russia to very little in the way of economic concessions
to Belarus. The result was a document that offered more integration than
the European Community, and perhaps—as Boris Yeltsin stated, than the
CIS—but significantly less than Gorbachev's formula for a revised USSR in
1991.

Prior to the signing of the Treaty, there was frantic activity and many hasty
amendments. On 31 March 1997, Ivan Rybkin, Russia's security chief,
arrived in Minsk, ostensibly to clarify certain issues with Lukashenka.
Lukashenka departed for Moscow not long after Rybkin had left. It was evident that Russia was dissatisfied with the original draft prepared in Minsk.
The new, three-page version, was described only as a "declaration of intent"
by the Russians, among whose delegates were evidently some of the pro-
western Russian elite. The truncated Russian version was accepted with surprising alacrity by the Belarusians, suggesting that the Belarusian delegation
at the Parliamentary Assembly had orders to accept any document that the
Russians ultimately put together. The process was too far advanced to be
stopped as the 2 April deadline loomed closer. The symbolism of a Union
Treaty on that date may have been of more significance than the Treaty
itself.[25]

The original Treaty declared that the two sides had proceeded "from the
spiritual affinity and community of the historic fates of their peoples...in
the interests of their social and economic progress." It contained nine brief
articles. The first stressed that the Community would be transformed into a
Union without the loss to either side of state sovereignty, independence,
territorial integrity, Constitution, coats of arms and other facets of statehood. The article undermined the content of the Union, which is too
all-encompassing a word: "association" would have been more appropri-
ate. Article 2 contained the crux of the treaty, and thus is worth citing in
full.

The aims of the Union are as follows: strengthening the relations of fraternity, friendship, and all-round cooperation between the Russian Federation and the Republic of Belarus in the political, economic, social, military, scientific, cultural, and other fields; improving the living standards of the people and creating favorable conditions for the all-round and harmonious development of the individual; ensuring the stable social and economic development of the member countries of the Union on the basis of the unification of their material and intellectual potential and the use of market mechanisms; bringing closer together their national legal systems and forming the legal system of the Union; ensuring security, maintaining a high level of defense capacity and jointly combatting crime; facilitating the maintenance of European security and development of mutually beneficial cooperation in Europe and in the world as a whole.[26]

Aside from the concept of a unified legal system, there was little here that did not exist in practice, albeit in a more modest version. Article 7 left open the possibility that other countries might join the Union, while Article 8 declared that the Treaty was of indefinite duration, though either side could withdraw from it by providing twelve months notice. The Treaty came into force from the date of its signing by the two presidents.

The Memorandum outlined the procedure for public discussion of the terms of the Treaty. This discussion was to take place from 2 April to 15 May. A joint commission was established to summarize the results of the discussion, co-chaired by Myasnikovich, the chief of the Belarusian president's administration, and V.M. Serov, the deputy chairman of the Russian government. Prime time television slots were assigned on Belarusian Television and Radio (i.e., state television and radio), ORT, VGTRK, and the Mayak radio station in Russia to debate the draft charter. The commission then had the task of submitting the results of the discussion to the two presidents on 20 May 1997. Within five days the draft charter would be forwarded to the Supreme Council of the Russia–Belarus Community to be ratified, together with the 2 April 1997 Treaty.[27]

The procedure seemed lengthy, but the time period was exceptionally brief for a Treaty of such apparent magnitude. The television debates provided some lighter moments. On one occasion a Russian interviewer ridiculed some members of the Belarusian delegation, many of whom appeared to be handpicked or members of the presidential administration. Lukashenka at this time (late April 1997) was on a tour of the Far East. Both sides hinted also that ultimately the Treaty would be subjected to national referenda. The Treaty appeared in general to be well accepted in both countries, though it was opposed by the BPF and many nationally conscious Belarusians. Despite the official propaganda touting the success of the Union and Lukashenka's new course for Belarus (having vanquished his enemies at home), there are reasons to think that the president was far from satisfied with the overall results. Belarus had in reality gained very little from the sacrifice of its neutrality.

On 12 June, after the exchange of documents the Union Parliamentary Assembly held its first session, held in Brest, evidently to erase the memory of the Belavezha agreement signed in the same region in 1991 dissolving the Soviet Union. The two sides wanted to adopt the tune of the former Soviet national anthem for the new Union, but with new lyrics; a decision immediately rejected by Boris Yeltsin. For Lukashenka, the immediate goals were no different from those of 1994–95, namely to secure an economic union as a priority before formalizing any sort of political union. As the assembly met, the Belarusian president was requesting payment from Russia of some RR1300 billion in promised credits, lower oil prices, and lower customs duties on Belarusian exports to Russia.[28] Rhetoric and personal sentiment had to take a back seat therefore to economic needs. There was no indication of how far the authority of the new assembly extended, and whether it was likely to wield real authority. In the Belarusian case, for example, the assembly could not overturn a presidential decree

Because of the frequency of Lukashenka's speeches and public appearances, it is hard for the observer to discern the integrity of policy and purpose of the Belarusian president. How, for example, could he hope to unite with Russia and retain Belarusian independence? If he did not join with Russia, then what was the purpose of the constant propaganda about rejoining the motherland or forming a new Slavic Union? What did the president really desire? Any answer to these questions has to be speculative, but some evidence is provided by a bizarre spectacle that occurred in Minsk in mid-March 1997 entitled the Congress of USSR Nations. This was the third such congress, following two similar events in Moscow, but in Belarus, as opposed to Russia, it was sponsored directly by the office of the president, and Lukashenka attended personally. He also made a speech, identifying his cause with that of the Communists—there to glorify Lenin and Stalin whose portraits were carried—and equated the forthcoming Union with his efforts to build a new structure in place of the Soviet Union. Some delegates denounced "traitors" such as Boris Yeltsin, while Lukashenka, who had already signed several treaties with Yeltsin, observed events without even a token protest.[29]

Though it is possible to read too much into such events—Lukashenka had not on this occasion advocated the reestablishment of the Soviet Union, which would have been well received in these circles—the fact that such a gathering was held at all under the auspices of the president's office indicates that Lukashenka looked favorably on the occasion. One could scarcely imagine his attendance at a BPF meeting, or even that of one of the centrist parties. Also, Lukashenka is a president who has a strong personal commitment to putting into practice his vision of society. He is not a bureaucrat, nor, like many Western leaders and indeed Soviet leaders such as Lenin and Gorbachev, did he begin his career in law. A farm chief from the Russified eastern regions of Belarus, his entire outlook is permeated by things Russian, the Soviet past, and the interests of the rural community, particularly farmers.

At the same time, Belarus and Russia did not share a common vision of a future society in 1997, though certain politicians in Russia—Zyuganov, for example, and possibly Zhirinovsky—may have held views similar to that of the Belarusian president. Lukashenka had created for himself a dominant position in Belarus. The country by the summer of 1997 was a presidential state that was approaching dictatorship. Yet it was a small stage for a man who liked the camera, ceremonial occasions, and particularly military parades and displays. All the same, had Russia resolved simply to annex Belarus, as a western province, Lukashenka's role in the newly expanded state could scarcely have been a major one. In short, the political posturing of Lukashenka and his maneuvers could only continue in an independent state. Paradoxically therefore, he could take the process only so far. It was akin to a man who reaches the cliff edge and realizes that he can go no further without breaking his neck.

Although Russia and Belarus had ratified in June the Act of Union signed on 2 April, neither side was committed to critical facets of any merger, such as a monetary union or the renunciation of sovereignty. In late September, the Belarusian president declared that he would never renounce Belarusian sovereignty, an indicator that relations between the two presidents had deteriorated. Some observers have suggested that Lukashenka's ultimate goal is to be the president of the Russian–Belarus Union, giving him authority over a vast territory stretching from the Polish border to the Pacific. There is little hard evidence to support such an assertion, and similarly little chance of such an event taking place, particularly as Lukashenka's popularity in Russia has dwindled. Nevertheless, the first three years of the Lukashenka presidency had seen a remarkable consolidation of authority in the office of the presidency.

THE ORT AFFAIR

In late July 1997, two prominent ORT journalists, Pavel Sheremet and Dmitry Zavadesky, were arrested and charged with illegally crossing the border into Belarus while putting together a report on smuggling. On 7 July, Sheremet was deprived of his press accreditation in Belarus, allegedly on the personal orders of Belarusian president. A further fifteen journalists were arrested in Minsk on 31 July for protesting the arrest of Sheremet and his detention in a KGB prison. On 28 July, the Minsk ORT offices were raided by the KGB, and among the items confiscated was Sheremet's passport. Subsequently, a second group of ORT journalists was detained on 15 August, including three Russians and one Belarusian citizen. The Belarusian authorities declared that the "incident" was a deliberate provocation, and that they had been tipped off by the Lithuanian authorities. Those arrested included the head of the Minsk bureau of the ORT, Dmitry Navazhylau, and Reuters correspondent, Andrey Makhouski.

On 18 August, another journalist, Valery Fashenka, was arrested for refusing to testify in the legal testimony against the ORT journalists, which began on this same day. On 22 August Fashenka was ordered expelled from Belarus. The decision to try to ban ORT from Belarus altogether was the logical culmination of the lengthy campaign to eliminate nongovernment media in Belarus, which began with the expulsion of Aleksandr Stupnikov in the spring of 1997. The crackdown was also a result of a new Law on the Press, which passed its first reading in the House of Representatives on 25 June, and which inter alia, would prohibit attacks on the president and centralize the media under a State Committee for the Press. The deputy chairman of the president's administration, Ivan Pashkevich, maintained that ORT had given a grossly inaccurate portrayal of the situation in Belarus. Previously, the president had maintained that camera shots shown on ORT of the beating of demonstrators the previous spring were fabricated.

Russian reaction, initially, was muted. Russian president, Boris Yeltsin, noted in early August that his Belarusian counterpart was young and hot tempered, but that the arrests would not adversely affect relations between the two states. Subsequently, his prime minister Viktor Chernomyrdin, and first deputy prime minister, Boris Nemtsov, demanded the release of the journalists. Nemtsov, a liberal democrat and a strong supporter of a market economy in Russia, was particularly scornful, comparing the situation in Belarus with that in Cuba or North Korea—the most scathing attack on the Lukashenka regime from a prominent politician in Russia to date. Russia belatedly took a firm stance on behalf of its citizens, and after some grumbling, Minsk released all the journalists except for Sheremet on 22 August. Sheremet was released in early October 1997 after Boris Yeltsin had refused permission for Lukashenka to visit two Russian provinces. However, the journalist was ordered to stay on Belarusian territory pending his trial.

OTHER STATES

Though relations with Russia have dominated Belarusian foreign policy, Lukashenka has not ignored other states, both neighbors, and states more distant. Relations with Ukraine remain cordial, at least outwardly. Lukashenka has met with his counterpart, Leonid Kuchma, on several occasions, including a two-day visit to Kiev on 12–13 May 1997. That meeting saw the signing of documents on economic cooperation, joint policies in dealing with the effects of the 1996 Chernobyl disaster, and other matters. Kuchma declined to criticize the Union agreement between Belarus and Russia, though he did not go as far as some eighty deputies in the Ukrainian parliament, who proposed that Ukraine should also agree to join.[30]

In April 1997, the Minsk press gave much publicity to President Lukashenka's visit to the Far East. On 22 April he arrived in Seoul in an attempt to promote business and trade ties between Belarus and South Korea. At the same time he expressed his support for peace talks that would accelerate peace with North Korea, and include the United States and China. Subsequently, he visited Vietnam to reduce the taxation on goods between the two countries and to discuss a treaty of friendship. This was the first visit of a leader of independent Belarus to Vietnam, though little of substance appears to have resulted from the various meetings, including one with Secretary-General of the Vietnamese Communist Party, Do Muo, on 24 April.[31]

Relations with other European countries have been more complex. The European Union has criticized the violations of the 1994 Constitution and the abuses of human rights that have taken place in Belarus under the administration of President Lukashenka. In a press release dated 29 April 1997, the EU expressed its "deep concern" at the arrests and detention of demonstrators, and dismissed the explanations offered by letters of 10 April from Lukashenka and Foreign Minister Antanovich. Following conclusions made during a fact-finding mission of 24 February 1997, the EU stated that there could be no cooperation between the EU and Belarus as long as the latter country failed to construct a political system that respected human rights and political freedoms. The EU offered its assistance in promoting a democratic society in Belarus, together with the OSCE and the Council of Europe.[32] Lithuania has been a focal point for the opposition, and Belarus has accused Lithuania on several occasions of border violations. In late 1997, a Belarusian military exercise caused concern in Vilnius when it crossed briefly into Lithuanian territory. There are no pressing border issues between the two countries, however.

On a more mundane level, despite an abortive effort by Scandinavian Airlines to offer a service to Minsk International, the main airport of Belarus is notable for its lack of foreign traffic, particularly when compared with its counterparts at Kiev and Moscow Sheremetyovo-2. Only Lufthansa, LOT, and Austrian Airlines offer a service from central Europe, and only the German airline arrives and departs on a daily basis. It is symbolic of the country's isolation from western Europe that to date not a single airline from this region has seen fit to commence a service to Minsk: neither from a tourist or a business perspective has it become economically viable or worthwhile.

CONCLUSION

Where does Belarus lie as the end of the 20th century approaches? Is there a future for this small nation of just over ten million people? How will it fit into the world of the 21st century? Will the Belarusian language and culture be extinct?

The present government is reflective of the current mindset of the older generation of the republic. The familiar disappeared after 1991 and the new insecurities were largely associated with the efforts of the first post-Soviet government to implement democratization, capitalism, and a market economy. At the head of the movement for reforms was the Belarusian Popular Front, led by the imposing figure of Zyanon Paznyak. The authorities turned on Paznyak and rendered him a virtual outlaw in his own country. He had a devout following, but it is doubtful if it encompassed more than 15% of the electorate at any one time. Paznyak, it was maintained by his enemies, was Russophobic, an extremist, a man who wanted to force a way of life that was alien to the majority of Belarusians. Another potential democratic leader, the physicist Stanislau Shushkevich, would forever be identified with the period when living standards for the majority of the population dropped sharply. In the final analysis, Shushkevich may have tried to satisfy too many parties, ultimately endearing himself to none of them.

It could be argued, then, that Lukashenka was offered the presidency as an alternative to the well-worn but ultimately corrupt Communist hierarchy, symbolized by prime minister Kebich, and the minority democrats who had never gained a firm hold over the general populace. Though the current president represents a particularly malevolent form of the late-Soviet mentality, he has introduced little that is new, either in the form of ideas or in material terms. Indeed, the most common phrase applied to Belarus, is that the country has returned "to the past." The Union with Russia is an apt symbol of this policy, whether or not the union is a reality or a paper fiction. Rallies such as May-Day and the 7 November anniversary are celebrated in Minsk as in no other city of the former Soviet Union. The new holiday, 3 July, once again returns the thoughts of citizens to the triumphs of the Great Patriotic War, a period when Belarus or the BSSR had been subject to some of the severest purges in the former empire, but also a period when the fearsome German Fascists were defeated. It is hardly a vision for the future.

Travelling frequently through Belarus over the past five years, this author has heard many disparaging comments about Lukashenka, but few from the older generation. Frequently he is praised as a strong leader, a leader for the time. In some quarters he is a virtual cult figure. Villages turn out to meet him, women weeping with adulation. If Lukashenka had not introduced a repressive society, he would be seen mainly as a man who symbolized the alleged benefits of the Soviet past. His power is almost complete.[33] Laws have become all-embracing and petty. Indeed people have been prosecuted for misdemeanors such as swearing in public. The poet and journalist Slavamir Adamovich was convicted under Article 188 of the Criminal Code of Belarus in June 1997 for composing a poem entitled "Kill the President."[34] Such words betray the frustration of that part of society which resents Lukashenka's growing authority and is relatively powerless to change things, particularly by way of the ballot box. The international community has often condemned the president's actions, but it can do little practical to assist those persecuted. The opposition is isolated and increasingly subjected to acts of vindictiveness and harassment.

The history of Belarus, however, suggests that the emerging nation will survive. Much depends on the younger generation, and those who experienced the national revival of the late 1980s. Belarus has a highly educated intellectual elite, with a good command of the national language, cosmopolitan and open to Western ideas. Contacts with the West have expanded rapidly since the late 1980s, despite official restrictions. Moreover, Belarus is not an island. It is encircled by neighbors, many of which are further ahead in the economic reform process, and especially the privatization of industry and agriculture, and all of which are further advanced in the creation of more democratic societies. The country is not immune to such influences. As we have suggested, even Russia has taken a radically different course, and it was precisely the freedom of expression permitted in Russia that so infuriated Lukashenka, when he witnessed television coverage of the attacks on demonstrators in Minsk. The perestroyka period has yielded some fruits.

The reform movement in Belarus will necessarily be a slow one. Moreover, it is dependent in part upon the continuing freedom of the younger generation to receive a broad education, to learn the national language, and to express its ideas. It is also hinged in part on the ability of the country to overcome an emerging demographic crisis, with a population decline, shortened lifespans, a poor health system, and generally unhealthy lifestyles, particularly among males. These are critical factors in the survival of any society. Belarusians have suffered more than most Europeans in this century. They have declared independence twice, and had a state thrust on them by the Soviet authorities which, by 1939, was significant in size and responded to the national aspirations of the past. National consciousness is less well developed than in neigboring states. What exists is often a Russified outlook, not in itself to be castigated, though it tends to carry a retrogressive outlook toward the political future. Russified or not, it remains distinctively Belarusian.

Ultimately, this writer feels, Belarus will survive and find its place in the world of the 21st century. The state will not disappear as a result of Chernobyl or demographic decline. And while economic reforms will undoubtedly bring economic hardship in the immediate future, there is no reason why they should not provide long term benefits. The transition will require control over corruption, moderation from the leadership (clearly absent at present), and a new conception of Belarus as a nation, which may correspond less to Paznyak's view of the future than to a combination of views of the Russophile community and the new intelligentsia. It will also necessitate some freedom of expression, and freedom of the press. Thus far the international community, including those offering financial aid and credits to Belarus, has not expressly tied aid to the observance of human rights, paying more attention to the national deficit than to the imprisonment of those expressing their views in public. Continuing repressions in the country are far more likely to continue if the West ignores them.

Whatever its limitations and whatever the idiosyncrasies of the present government, independent Belarus has survived for six years. The opposition is far from cowed and the country may be on the road to dictatorship, but it is as yet some way from achieving this status. In the summer of 1997, for example, as has been described above, the regime continued its crackdown against journalists from the Russian ORT station, arresting six of them. When Russia reacted strongly, however, all were eventually released, an indicator that Lukashenka cannot work in isolation, but must pay attention to the wishes of his Russian partner. For this reason, this writer believes that those democrats who wish for and even insist on the breaking of all ties between Belarus and Russia—they focus on Russian imperialism and its sinister designs on Belarus—are committing a cardinal error. Links with like-minded democrats in Russia are essential if Belarus is to emerge from the current repressive government.

In short, contacts with Russia are inevitable, but they need not be linked to Russian "imperial" interests. Further, even Lukashenka has maintained contacts with other neighboring states, particularly with the presidents of Poland and Ukraine, and with the states of Southeast Asia. Lukashenka has also made arrangements for a special consultative relationship with NATO, on a similar basis to that in Ukraine. Even though in theory, the Belarusian government is hostile to the eastward expansion of NATO and has stated so on several occasions, it has not broken off contacts and negotiations either with NATO or the European Union. The OSCE has debated opening a permanent office in Minsk, again despite the difficulties of dealing with an obdurate and harsh presidential regime.

It is clear that the United States has no wish to deepen its relationship with the current government of Belarus. Outgoing ambassador Kenneth Yalowitz made the US government's dissatisfaction clear in his farewell speech from the Minsk embassy in 1997. But Lukashenka has always liked a larger stage and is unlikely to isolate Belarus. There is no reason why Belarus should disappear from the map of Europe.

Finally, will Lukashenka survive? The question has loomed almost as large as that about the future of Belarus, such has been the impact of the president over his first three years in office. President Lukashenka remains secure however, because of the following factors:

1. Belarus remains a critical military and security base for Russia; in addition to being a conduit for oil, and for potential links to the distant Kaliningrad region. Whatever his idiosyncrasies, Lukashenka is an important ally to Russia, particularly in view of the Russophobic statements of the main Belarusian opposition leaders in recent months. In view of the forthcoming expansion of NATO into Poland, Hungary and the Czech Republic, and the neutrality of Ukraine, it is vital for Russia to have a stable ally in Minsk.

2. Though isolated, and with declining foreign investment, Belarus is not on the verge of economic collapse. While the country is witnessing increased impoverishment, a plethora of scapegoats has been found, not least privatization and the attempted isolation of the country by the IMF and other financial institutions. The opening of the new Ford plant, the expansion of McDonald's, a thriving foreign car market, and other factors all suggest that the country is not another North Korea. The economic decline is evident, but it is gradual and masked by official propaganda and distorted statistics.

3. Recent polls suggest that Lukashenka remains by far the most popular politician in Belarus, with the support of about 45% of the electorate. None of the opposition figures have reached double figures; none have

the national credibility and standing required to pose a serious threat to Lukashenka, even if one assumes that the president may make a concession to his opponents and hold a presidential election in 1999, as warranted by the constitution in force at the time he took office. Moreover, the opposition appears to have seriously limited its options by either focusing on policies that perceive Russia as the principal enemy of Belarusian independence (the BPF), or on constitutional issues rather than economic ones (the United Civic Party).

4. The president has emphasized the importance of two sectors of society in particular: the farmers and the military. The former have been recipients of prose more reminiscent of the laudations of peasants offered by 19th century Russian populists than a late 20th century political leader. The president has a distrust of the urban intellectual, which is contrasted with the "natural goodness" of the rural resident with his attachment to the soil. This idiosyncrasy of the Belarusian leader renders false the comparisons with Stalin that are frequently made by the opposition. Whereas Stalin possessed an instrinsic distrust of the peasant, Lukashenka has made him the prop for his regime.

    The army's exact numbers are not known, but it has expanded recently, and was widely believed to exceed 100,000 in 1997. Minsk in the summer of 1997 was notable for the presence of army vehicles and militia in virtually every sector of the city. Army Day has once again become a major event in the Belarusian calendar, and the president has relied on both the presidential guard and the militia to break up demonstrations. Allied to his allocation of a significant role to the army has been the increased activity of the KGB, which has been used to conduct systematic investigations of real and imagined opponents of the regime. As the farmer provides electoral support for the Lukashenka regime, so the army constitutes the foundation of the system. As long as it remains loyal to the president, there is little possibility of change from within the country.

5. As I have argued in this book and elsewhere,[35] the Lukashenka presidency is consolidated, but it does not yet penetrate all walks of life. It still possible—though difficult—to operate newspapers that are critical of the president. The political system possesses too many loopholes and inefficiencies to constitute an all-pervasive regime that can sweep down on its opponents. It is nonetheless one of the most repressive states of Europe and functions according to a revised constitution founded on the basis of a spurious referendum. The two major bugbears of the past for Lukashenka—the parliament and the Constitutional Court—no longer exist in their original form.

The historian might perceive the Belarusian government as the result of a period of upheaval and political and economic uncertainty, the periodic reversion to strong leadership and rhetoric that looks with nostalgia on the certainties and stability of the late Soviet regime. These same factors, however, apply to all the post-Soviet governments. With the possible exception of the brief sojourn of President Gamsakhurdia in Georgia, none has produced a Lukashenka. Belarus has clung to the past and accepted gross violations of democracy and its constitution at a time of change in its neighboring states. Economically, Russia and Poland today have more in common than Russia and Belarus.

The historian might also argue that all the surrounding countries have a more widely advanced national consciousness than exists currently within Belarus. All ultimately wish to pursue the process of nation-building, despite economic problems, rampant corruption, and frequent political upheavals (as I write, for example, there is a move from within the Ukrainian parliament to impeach President Leonid Kuchma, and there is no agreement between the Ukrainian president and his parliament on budget priorities for 1998). He might also note that the most important catalyst of political change in Belarus in the recent past has been Russia—1917, 1922, 1926, 1939, 1991, for example, are all years that wrought profound political changes in Belarus that originated in Russia. The states of Europe do not have a monopoly on democratization, and there is no reason why Belarus should not be influenced in this direction from unexpected quarters. Once again the main impetus for change in Belarus may come not from the democratic states of western and central Europe, but from the former colonial and Soviet ruler, and present-day affirmed friend, Russia. It seems inexplicable that Belarusian democrats, and particularly the BPF, have thus far not only explored this outlet, but have dismissed Russia entirely, as an exploiting and exploitative nation; overlooking in the process some very fundamental changes and new directions that are applicable to the Eastern neighbor. Too often in conversations with democratic-minded people in Belarus, this author has been informed that there is no possibility of an early end to the present repressive and intrusive regime with its unpredictable leader. Yet there is. There can be no reversion to the Soviet era without Russia, and for many Russians there is simply no road back to the past. As this book has indicated, politics have taken priority over economics in Belarus over the past four years, if not throughout the period of independence. The ruling elite today had at least a foothold in the hierarchy in the Soviet period. They have proven largely incapable of dealing with the most pressing questions, with profound changes in

eastern Europe, or of moderating the actions of the presidential administration.

1   Press release of the Embassy of the Republic of Belarus in the United States, cited in *Belarusian Review*, Vol. 6, No. 4 (Winter 1994–95): 20.
2   See, for example, Kenneth S. Yalowitz, "The U.S. and Belarus: Challenges and Opportunities," *Belarusian Review*, Vol. 8, No. 2, Summer 1996, p. 4.
3   OMRI Daily Report, 31 October 1995; and 1 November 1995.
4   OMRI Daily Report, 10 June 1996.
5   OMRI Daily Report, 7 July 1995; *Izvestiya*, 6 July 1995.
6   Monitor, 19 January 1996.
7   *Minsk Economic News*, No. 23, December 1996, p. 2.
8   David R. Marples, "Belarus: Prospects for 1995," Oxford Analytica Research Brief, December 1994.
9   The currency was named after the hare depicted on the bill.
10 Alexander Burda, "Rouble Zone: To Be Or Not To Be?" *Minsk Economic News*, No. 5, May 1994, p. 1.
11 *Belarusian Review*, Vol. 6, No. 3 (Fall 1994): 3; and *The Washington Post*, 10 September 1994.
12 Reuters, 6 January 1995.
13 Reuters, 22 February 1995; Interfax, 23 February 1995.
14 Reuters, 17 November 1995.
15 Reuters, 28 February 1996; OMRI Daily Report, 28 February 1996.
16 *Belarusian Review*, Vol. 8, No. 1 (Spring 1996): 7–8.
17 David R. Marples, "Belarusian-Russian Treaty: An Analysis," *Belarusian Review*, Vol. 8, No. 1 (Spring 1996): 8–9.
18 Nikolay Musienko, "Vetbi odnogo dereva: podpisan dogovor mezhu Rossiey i Belorussiey," *Pravda*, April 3, 1996, p. 1.
19 *Rossiiskaya gazeta*, 13 April 1996.
20 OMRI Daily Report, 16 April 1996.
21 Interfax, 25 June 1996.
22 Interfax, 25 June 1996; OMRI Daily Report, 24 July 1996.
23 Belarusian Television, 24 July 1996.
24 David R. Marples, "Belarus: Prospects for 1997," Oxford Analytica Research Brief, December 1996.
25 Tatiana Kalinovskaya, "Treaty's Importance Overstated," *Minsk Economic News*, No. 7, April 1997, p. 2; *Narodnaya volya*, 4 April 1997, p. 1.
26 *Rossiiskaya gazeta*, 3 April 1997.
27 Ibid.
28 "Belarus Between Dialogue and Polarization," *The Jamestown Foundation Prism*, Vol. III, No. 10, Part 1, 27 June 1997.
29 See, for example, Valery Kalinovsky, "President Pleases the Nostalgic," *Minsk Economic News*, No. 6, March 1997, p. 1.
30 RFE/RL Newsline, 13 May 1997.
31 Ibid., 24 April 1997.
32 The press release is cited in *Belarusian Review*, Vol. 9, No. 2 (Summer 1997): 7–8.
33 Lukashenka is not a dictator in the modern sense of the word in that his term in office is still limited by the Constitution. According to the revised version, no president can remain office for more than two terms. Hence, barring further revisions to the Constitution, is term in office expires in the year 2006, at which time he would be only 51 years old, younger than Mikhail Gorbachev when he first became General Secretary of the CC CPSU in March 1985.
34 *Chatsvertaya ulada*, No. 5 (1997): 5.
35 David R. Marples, "Belarus: An Analysis of the Lukashenka Regime." *The Harriman Review*, Vol. 10, No. 1 (Spring 1997): 24–28.

Bibliography

Academy of Sciences BSSR. Institute of Art, Ethnography, and Folklore. *Cultural Policy in the Byelorussian Soviet Socialist Republic*. Paris, 1979.

Bolotnikova, Larisa. "Investment Trends in Belarus." *Minsk Economic News*, No. 5 (March 1995).

Burda, Alexander. "Rouble Zone: To Be Or Not To Be?" *Minsk Economic News*, No. 5 (May 1994).

Byelorussian Soviet Socialist Republic (BSSR), Mission to the United Nations, "Statement by Pyotr K. Krauchanka, Minister for Foreign Affairs of the Byelorussian SSR, on agenda item 14 'Report of the International Atomic Energy Agency,'" at the 45th session of the United Nations General Assembly, New York, 23 October 1990.

Current Digest of the Soviet Press, *Current Soviet Policies VI: The Documentary Record of the 24th Congress of the Communist Party of the Soviet Union*. Compiled by Richard Bessel. Columbus, Ohio: America Association for the Advancement of Slavic Studies, 1973.

Drakokhrust, Yuri. "Referendum: New Era Begins." *Minsk Economic News*, No. 23, December 1996.

Dziabola, Mikola. "Inflation Programmed into New Budget." *Belarusian Review*, Vol. 7, No. 1 (Spring 1995).

Guthier, Steven L. "The Belorussians: National Identification and Assimilation, 1897–1970. Part 1, 1897–1939." *Soviet Studies*, Vol. XXIX, No. 1 (January 1977): 37–61.

Iwanow, Mikolaj. "The Byelorussians of Eastern Poland under Soviet Occupation." In Keith Sword, ed., *The Soviet Takeover of the Polish Eastern Provinces, 1939–41* (London: The Macmillan Press, 1991), pp. 253–267.

Kabysh, Symon. "Genocide of the Byelorussians." In Vitaut Kipel and Zora Kipel, eds., *Byelorussian Statehood: Reader and Bibliography* (New York: Byelorussian Institute of Arts and Sciences), pp. 229–243.

Kalinovskaya, Tatiana. "Treaty's Importance Overstated." *Minsk Economic News*, No. 7, April 1997.

Kalinovsky, Valery. "President Pleases the Nostalgic." *Minsk Economic News*, No. 6, March 1997.

Knight, Amy. *Beria: Stalin's First Lieutenant*. Princeton, N.J.: Princeton University Press, 1993.

Knight, Amy. "Pyotr Masherov and the Soviet Leadership: A Study in Kremlinology." *Survey*, Vol. 26, No. 1 (Winter 1982).

Krawchenko, Bohdan, ed., *Ukraine After Shelest*. Edmonton: Canadian Institute of Ukrainian Studies, 1983.

Kuchinsky, G. "Lord Created Us Centrist." *Minsk Economic News*, No. 3, March 1993.

Letters to Gorbachev: New Documents from Soviet Byelorussia. London: The Association of Byelorussians in Great Britain, 1987.

Lucas, Edward. "Belarus Out of the Slow Lane." *Belarusian Review*, Vol. 6, No. 4 (Winter 1994/95).

Mamenok, Tatiana. "Privatisation Slow and Erratic." *Minsk Economic News*, No. 21 (November 1996).

Markus, Ustina. "The Russian-Belarusian Monetary Union." *RFE/RL Research Report*, Vol. 3, No. 20, 20 May 1994.

Markus, Ustina. "Siamion Sarecki, New Parliament Speaker." *Belarusian Review*, Vol. 8, No. 1 (Spring 1996).

Marples, David R. "Belarus: An Analysis of the Lukashenka Regime." *The Harriman Review*, Vol. 10, No. 1 (Spring 1997): 24–28.

Marples, David R. *Belarus: From Soviet Rule to Nuclear Catastrophe*. Basingstoke, UK: The Macmillan Press, 1996.

Marples, David R. "Belarus: The New Dictatorship of Eastern Europe?" *Belarusian Review*, Vol. 9, No. 1 (Spring 1997).

Marples, David R. "Belarus: The Politics of the Presidency." *Belarusian Review*, Vol. 7, No. 2 (Summer 1995).

Marples, David R. "Belarus: Prospects for 1995." Oxford Analytica Research Brief, December 1994.

Marples, David R. "Belarus: Prospects for 1996." Oxford Analytica Research Brief, December 1996.

Marples, David R. "Belarus: Prospects for 1997." Oxford Analytica Research Brief, December 1996.

Marples, David R. "Belarusian-Russian Treaty: An Analysis." *Belarusian Review*, Vol. 8, No. 1 (Spring 1996).

Marples, David R. "More Demonstrations and Arrests in Belarus." Oxford Analytica Research brief, May 1996.

Marples, David. "Presidential Elections: The View From Miensk." *Belarusian Review*, Vol. 6, No. 1 (Spring 1994).

Mienski, J. "The Establishment of the Belorussian SSR." *Belorussian Review*, No. 1 (1955).

Shchukin, Leonid. "Joint Ventures." *Minsk Economic News*, No. 4, April 1993.

Solchanyk, Roman. "The Study of the Russian Language in Belorussia." *Radio Liberty Research Bulletin*, RL 30/80, 21 January 1980.

Thompson, John M. *A Vision Unfulfilled: Russia and the Soviet Union in the Twentieth Century*. Toronto: D.C. Heath and Co., 1996.

Turevich, Art. "Byelorussia: Genocide of a Nation, Part II." *Byelorussian Review*, Vol. 1, No. 4–5 (Winter 1989–90).

Turevich, Art. "Byelorussia's Declaration of Sovereignty: Its Meaning." *Belarusian Review*, Vol. 2, No. 3 (Fall 1990).

Turevich, Art. "Elections in Belarus: Their Meaning." *Belarusian Review*, Vol. 7, No. 2 (Summer 1995).

Urban, Michael and Jan Zaprudnik, "Belarus: A Long Road to Nationhood." In Ian Bremmer and Ray Taras, eds., *Nations and Politics in the Soviet Successor States* (Cambridge: Cambridge University Press, 1993).

Vakar, Nicholas P. *Belorussia: The Making of a Nation*. Cambridge, Mass.: Harvard University Press, 1954.

Yakovlevsky, Roman. "Faces and Images." *Minsk Economic News*, No. 4, April 1993.

Yalowitz, Kenneth S. "The U.S. and Belarus: Challenges and Opportunities." *Belarusian Review*, Vol. 8, No. 2, Summer 1996.

Zaprudnik. *Belarus: At A Crossroads in History*. Boulder, Co: The Westview Press, 1993.

Index

Abramovich, Alyaksandr, 82
Adamovich, Ales, 49
Adamovich, Slavamir, 122
Agrarian Party of Belarus, 73, 76, 80
Aleksey II (Patriarch of Moscow), 113
Alexandrov, Serge, 101–102
All-Belarusian Association of Poets
    and Writers (*Maladnyak*), 7
All-Belarusian Congress (1944), 17
Andropov, Yuri, 71
Antanovich, Ivan, 120
Armenia, Armenians, 63
Army (military), 125
Arochka, N.N., 66n
Asipovichy, 11
Astrouski, Radislau, 17
Austria, 34
Austrian Airlines, 121
Austro-Hungarian Empire, 3
Azerbaidzhan, 42–43, 63

Babruisk, 2, 10
Baevo (Vitsebsk Oblast), 33
Bahdankevich, Stanislau, 34, 37,
    72, 77, 79–80
Baltic states, 3–4
Baranavichi (oblast), 14, 111
Barouski, A., 16
Barysava-Osipava, Maryya, 56–57
Bazhelka, Aleh, 100
Belarus:
    Belarusianization in the 1920s,
        6–8
    Belarusianization in Western
        Belarus, 14
    collectivization of agriculture, 9–11
    constitutional crisis (November
        1996), 93–99

cultural revival, 2, 6–8
declaration of independence
    in 1918; 3–5
declaration of independence
    in 1991, 58–60
declaration of state sovereignty, 59
demographic makeup, 2, 11,
    30–31, 51–52
destruction of national elite and
    culture, 8–9, 18–19
early postwar years, 17–19
early Stalinism, 8–9
economy, 1986–96, 27–45
German invasion, 15–17
incorporation of Western
    Belarus, 12–15
industrial development
    in 1930s, 11–12
Kurapaty revelations in, 54–58
language issue in, 50–54
Masherau years, 19–23
November 1996 crisis, 93–99
and nuclear nonproliferation,
    107–108
passivity in, 65
referendum of spring 1995, 72–75
referendum of November 1996,
    96–99
relations with Russia, 107–119
relations with Ukraine,
    other states, 120–121
unemployment in, 39–40
union with Russia, 43, 115–118
Belarusbank, 100
Belarusian Academy of Sciences,
    8, 55, 110
Belarusian Association of
    Peasants, 13

Belarusian Autocephalous
   Orthodox Church, 17
Belarusian Central Council, 17
Belarusian Charitable Fund "For the
   Children of Chernobyl," 100–101
Belarusian Christian Democratic
   Party, 13, 48, 80
Belarusian Committee (Prague), 16
Belarusian Communist Party
   (see Communist Party of Belarus)
Belarusian Council (Vilna), 4–5
Belarusian Council of
   Ministers, 50, 62
Belarusian Government-in-Exile
   (Prague), 8
Belarusian Land Defense, 17
Belarusian National Association, 13
Belarusian National Republic (BNR),
   4, 8, 49
BNR Rada, 4, 17
Belarusian Nationalist Party, 16
Belarusian Patriotic Movement, 76
Belarusian Peasants Party, 76
Belarusian Popular Front (BPF), 5,
   33, 57, 59, 62–64, 66, 70, 72,
   76, 80, 90, 101, 103, 121
   activities in 1996–97, 99
   campaigns for new parliamentary
      elections, 73
   conflict with government, 83–85,
      104
   defends 1994 Constitution, 82
   formation of, 47–50
   forms political party, 61
   Russophobia of, 125–127
   and Union Treaty, 116
Belarusian Revolutionary Party (see
   Belarusian Socialist Hramada)
Belarusian Rights Protection
   Committee, 100
Belarusian Self-Aid Committee, 16
Belarusian Social Democratic
   Party, 3

Belarusian Social Revolutionary
   Party, 4
Belarusian Socialist Hramada, 3,
   4, 5, 13
Belarusian Socialist Party, 76
Belarusian Soros Foundation, 100
Belarusian Soviet Socialist Republic
   (BSSR), 5–8, 13–14, 18
BSSR Supreme Soviet, 13, 18, 53,
   58, 61, 84, 125
   and the Community of Sovereign
      Republics, 113
   elections of 1995, 76–77
BSSR Trading and Industrial
   Chamber, 55
Belarusian State Library, 7
Belarusian State Press Committee, 81
Belarusian State University, 7, 53
Belarusian TV, 94, 116
Belaruskaya delovaya gazeta, 81, 91
Belaruskaya gazeta, 91
Belaruskaya presa, 81
Belaruskiy rynok, 91
Belavezha agreement, 61, 71, 107, 117
Belaya Rus Slavic Congress
*Belorusskaya Sovetskaya
   Entsiklopediya*, 56
Bereza Kartuska, 7
Berezina River, 16
Beria, L.P., 25n
Bialystok, 13, 16, 18
Black Sea Fleet, 109
Bolshakov, Aleksey, 112, 114
Bolshevik Party, 4–5
Bolshevik Revolution (see October
   Revolution)
Brazauskas, Algirdas, 110
Brest, 5, 13–14, 18, 29–30 (see also
   Brest-Litovsk and Treaty of
   Brest-Litovsk)
Brezhnev, L.I., 20–22, 26n
Bykau, Vasil, 49, 66n
Byrne, Peter, 100

Camdessus, Michel, 36
Canada, 34, 110
Carter, Ashton, 108
Catholics, Catholicism, 7
Central Election Commission, 91
Central Intelligence Agency (CIA),
 114
Central Powers (Germany and
 Austria-Hungary), 3
Charter of the Belarus-Russia
 Union, 115
Chechnya, Chechens, 83, 109
Chernenko, Konstantin, 22
Chernobyl disaster, 27–30, 32–33,
 43, 49, 83, 101, 103, 120
Chernomyrdin, Viktor, 72, 95,
 110, 112, 119
Children of Chernobyl Fund (see
 Belarusian Charitable Fund
 "For the Children of
 Chernobyl")
Children of the Lie, 49
China, 120
Chumakou, Alyaksandr, 109
Chyhir, Mikhail, 71–72, 94, 111
Citihope International, 101
Civic Action, 79–80
collectivization, 8–11, 14, 18
Collins, James, 108
Committee for the Defense of
 the Western Belarusian
 Hramada, 8
Committee for State Security
 (KGB), 48, 98, 100–101,
 105n, 119, 125
Commonwealth of Independent
 States (CIS), 61–63
Communist Party of Belarus, 3, 5,
 8, 9, 15, 16, 47, 58–60, 73,
 76, 80
Communist Party of Poland (KPP), 7
Communist Party of Western Belarus
 (KPZB), 5, 7, 8

Communists for Democracy, 71
Community of Sovereign Republics
 (CSR), 112–114
Congress of USSR Nations, 117
Constitution of 1994, 69, 72, 74,
 79–80, 82, 86, 89–90, 92, 99,
 107–108, 120
Constitution of 1996–97, 92–93,
 99, 103
Constitutional Court, 79, 86,
 93, 95, 97–99, 125
Conventional Armed Forces in
 Europe (CFE) Treaty, 108
Council of Europe, 120
Council of the Republic, 89,
 98–99, 105n
Curzon Line, 18
Czechoslovakia (Czech Republic),
 3, 124

De Gaulle, Charles, 93
Democratic Opposition, 64
Demokratychna Ukraina, 81
Dmowski, Roman, 7
Dnyapro River, 32
Dregovichi, 1
Dubko, Alyaksandr, 69–70
Dubrovno, 33
Dvina River, 1
Dzerzhinski, Feliks, 71
Dzyuba, Uladzimir, 83

Economic Court, 98
economic development, 27–45
energy, 32–34, 42
Estonia, 3, 59
European Union (EU), 98,
 120, 124

Fadzeyau, Valery, 91
Fashenka, Valery, 119
February Revolution of
 1917, 3

Federation of Belarusian Trade
    Unions, 36
Filaret, 113
First All-Belarusian Congress,
    5
First Belarusian National
    Congress, 91
First Five-Year Plan, 8,
    10, 11
First World War, 3–4
Ford plant, 124
Franckel, Alan, 78
Frantishak Skaryna Society
    of the Belarusian Language,
    53

Gamsakhurdia, Zviad, 126
Gazprom, 111
Germany, Germans, 4–5, 15–17,
    34, 43, 55–58, 77, 79, 91
Gorbachev, M.S., 27, 47, 52,
    54, 112, 115, 118
Gorelik, Yevgeniy, 67n
Government Commission
    (Kurapaty), 55–57
Grand Duchy of Lithuania, 1, 3, 14
"Great Patriotic War," 15–18,
    122
Green Party, 76
Gusarev, N., 18
Guthier, Steven, 2

Halko, Mikola, 81
Hanchar, Viktar, 91, 94
Hancharyk, Uladzimir, 36
Hitler, Adolf, 16–17, 78–79, 104
Homel (city), 2, 11, 15, 51
Homel (oblast), 6, 10, 29, 39, 98
House of Representatives, 89,
    98, 119
Hramyka, Uladzimir, 102
Hrodna (city), 91
Hrodna (oblast), 29–30, 102–103

Hrushavaya, Iryna, 101
Hrushavy, Henadz, 59, 65, 93, 101
Hryb, Mechyslau, 73–74, 76–77,
    80, 103
Hryshan, Ihar, 63
Hungary, 108, 124

Ihnatouski, U.M., 8, 9
Ilyukhin, Viktor, 114
Imya, 91, 98
India, Indians, 52
industry, 8, 10, 11, 20
Institute of Belarusian Culture
    (Minsk), 7
Institute of Legal Expertise
    (BSSR Ministry of Justice),
    55
Inter-Bank Accounting Center, 38
International Helsinki Federation
    for Human Rights, 84
International Monetary Fund
    (IMF), 33, 35–37, 124
Italy, 34

Jewish Bund, 3, 4
Jews, 2, 13, 16, 51, 56

Kaliningrad (oblast), 112, 114, 124
Kalinouski, Kastus, 1–2
Kalyakin, Syarhey, 80
Kapitan, Vasil, 100
Kapitula, Pyotr, 38
Karaleu (Mr.), 74
Karpenka, Henadz, 42, 69,
    79, 90, 101
Kasperovich, G.I., 52
Kazakhs, Kazakhstan, 22, 42–43,
    62–63, 108, 111–112
Kebich, Vyachaslau, 59–64, 67n,
    69–70, 76, 107, 110, 121
KGB (see Committee for State Security)
Khadyka, Yury, 48, 83–84
Khasbulatov, Ruslan, 67n

Khrushchev, Nikita S., 26n
Khryukin, T.T., 18
khutors, 9
Kiev (Kyiv), 1, 82–83, 121
Kievan Rus', 1
Knight, Amy, 21–22
Kolas, Yakub, 7
Kommunist Belorussii, 53
Kosygin, A.I., 20–21, 26n
Krauchanka, Pyotr, 28, 77
Kravchuk, Leonid, 61
Krivichi, 1
Krychau (city), 11
Kube, Wilhelm, 17
Kuchma, Leonid, 72–73,
    107, 110, 120, 126
kulaks (dekulakization), 9–10, 18
Kupala, Yanka, 7, 8
Kurapaty, 8–9, 49, 54–58
Kyrgyzstan, 43, 112

Lastouski, Vaslau, 8
Latvia, 4, 59
Law on the Press, 119
League for the Liberation
    of Belarus, 8
Lebed, Aleksandr, 107
Lenin, V.I., 6, 9, 54, 65, 117–118
Lida (city), 16, 108–109
Linh, Syarhey, 71, 94, 111
Lit-Bel, 5
Lithuania, Lithuanians, 1, 4, 14,
    16, 47, 49, 80, 119–120
LOT (Polish airlines), 121
Lufthansa (German airlines), 121
Lukashenka, Alyaksandr, 3, 5,
    37–38, 40, 80, 86
    amends Constitution, 89–93
    background of, 70–71
    and Belarusian Popular Front, 85
    dictatorship of, 127n
    economy under, 35–45
    and elections of 1995, 76

and *Handelsblatt* interview,
    78–79
and the media, 80–81
and older generation, 122
and NATO, 108–109
offensives of spring 1997,
    99–104
presidential election
    campaign, 69–70, 121
prospects for future, 124–125
referendum of 1995, 73–75
referendum of November 1996,
    93–99
and Russia (CSR and Union),
    107–117
and the Russian language, 78
and Soviet textbooks, 77
speeches of, 72
vision of society, 104, 118
visit to Far East, 120
Lutskevich brothers, 2
Luzin, Anatol, 83

Machine-Tractor Stations, 10, 18
Mahileu (city), 2, 11, 51
Mahileu (oblast), 10, 29
Makhouski, Andrey, 119
Malafeyeu, Anatol, 98
Maldzis, Adam, 53
Maltseu, Leanid, 91, 105n
Martyrolog of Belarus, 47, 57
Marxism, 2–3
Masherau, P.M., 19–23, 25n, 65, 71
Masherauvaya, Yelena, 21
Matskevich, Uladzimir, 105n
Mayak radio station (Moscow), 116
MAZ truck factory, 111
Mazay, N.N., 55
Mazurau, K.T., 19–22
Mazyr (city), 15
Mazyr (region), 10
McDonald's, 124
Minkevich, Mikhail, 23

Minsk (city), 2, 3, 6, 14,
16, 17, 23, 31, 91;
becomes capital of BSSR, 5
becomes Hero City, 22
Belarusian Popular Front in, 47
demonstrations and protests in,
35–36, 64, 83–84, 94, 113
falls to Germans in 1941, 15
growth of, 51
and Referendum of 1996, 98
unemployment in, 39
Minsk (oblast), 10, 29
Minsk Economic News, 82
Minsk International Airport,
120–121
Minsk State and University
Library (see Belarusian
State Library)
Molotov, V.I., 14
Molotov-Ribbentrop Treaty, 12
Moore, Rev. Paul, 101
Muo, Do, 120
My i vremya, 67n
Myasnikovich, Mikhail, 71, 112, 116

Nadezhda Express, 101
Narodnaya hazeta, 67n, 73, 81–82
Nash Kompas, 67n
Nasha Niva, 2
National Bank of Belarus, 35–36,
38, 100
National Centre of Strategic
Initiatives "East-West," 100
Navazhylau, Dmitry, 119
Navumchyk, Syarhey, 90
Nemtsov, Boris, 119
New Economic Policy, 9
Nineteenth Party Conference
(CPSU), 47
NKVD, 9, 15, 25n, 55–58, 67n
Nonproliferation Treaty, 108
NATO Partnership for Peace
Program, 108, 124

North Korea, 120
Novikau, Vasil, 69–70
NTV (Moscow), 84, 93, 102
Nunn-Lugar Program, 108

October Revolution of 1917, 2
Organization for Security and
Cooperation in Europe
(OSCE), 98, 120
OMON, 84, 103
Open Media Research
Institute, 113
ORT (Moscow), 93,
104, 116,
"ORT Affair," 118–119,
123

Pan-Slavic Congress, 37
partisans, 15–17, 19–20,
25n, 56
Party of Communists of
Belarus, 59
Party of Freedom, 84
Party of Public Accord, 76
Pashkevich, Ivan, 102, 119
Patolichev, N., 18
Paznyak, Zyanon, 54–55, 57–58,
62–63, 66n, 67n, 76, 99, 110,
121, 123
applies for asylum in
the United States, 90
background of, 48–49
conflicts with Lukashenka,
85, 105n
hunger strike of, 74
in Kiev, 82–83, 113
presidential election
campaign of, 69–70
People's Assembly of Western
Belarus, 13–14
Pilsudski, Josef, 7
Pinsk, 2, 14
Podgorny, N.V., 22, 26n

Poland, Poles, 1, 2, 3, 4, 5,
7, 8, 12–15, 18, 32,
34, 43, 102–103, 108,
112, 124, 126
Polatsk, 1
Polish-Soviet War (1920), 5–6
Ponomarenko, P., 18
population (see Belarus,
demographic situation)
population exchange (1944–48), 18
Pravda, 10, 112–113
Pripyat River, 1
privatization, 33–34, 39
Pryshchepa, D.F., 9

Radimichi, 1
Radyanska Ukraina , 81
Rahneda, 1
Rahvalod (Prince), 1
Rechytsa (district), 6
Red Army, 5, 12–13, 16
Referendum of November 1996,
96–99
Rodionov, Igor, 109
Rokossovsky, K.K., 16, 18
Russia, Russians, 2, 3, 6,
27–28, 32, 42–43, 49–51,
64, 72, 95, 108, 126;
and Community of Sovereign
Republics with Belarus
(CSR), 41, 82, 95, 112, 116
complains at treatment of
citizens by Belarus, 102
customs union/economic
integration with Belarus,
41–42, 74–75, 111
declares independence, 59
intervention in November 1996
referendum, 95–96, 98–99
military-security union with
Belarus, 62–63
monetary union with Belarus,
34–35, 110

Treaty of Friendship and
Cooperation with Belarus, 111
Treaty of Friendship and
Cooperation with Ukraine, 109
Union with Belarus, 102,
104, 114, 115–118, 121
Russia-Belarus Parliamentary
Assembly, 113–114, 117
Russian Duma, 98, 113
Russian Social Democratic
Workers' Party, 2–3
Russification, 22–23, 50–52,
107, 123
Rybkin, Ivan, 115
Rzecz Pospolita, 1

St. Petersburg, 3
Saredzich, Iosif, 73
Scandinavian Airlines, 120–121
Second Five-Year Plan, 11–12
Senka, Uladzimir, 71–72
Serlechnikov, Gennadiy, 95
Serov, V.M., 116
Sharetski, Syamen, 80, 82,
84–86, 114
and the November
1996 crisis, 90–96, 98
Shcherbytsky, Volodymyr, 21
Shchukin, Valery, 102
Shelest, Petro, 21
Sheremet, Pavel, 118–119
Sheremetyovo-2 airport
(Moscow), 121
Sholodanov, V., 58
Shushkevich, Stanislau,
60–66, 67n, 69–70, 75–76,
92, 103, 107, 121
Shyrkouski, E.I., 55
Sianko, Uladzimir, 108
Siuchyk, Vyachaslau, 84
Skaryna, Frantsishak, 1
Slavs, 1
Slutsk (city), 16

Smalenski, A., 53
Smolensk, 1, 5–6
Sobolev, Valeriy, 67n
Social Democratic Hramada, 76, 90
Society of Belarusian Language, 100
Soros, George, 100–101
Sovetskaya Belorussiya, 22, 63,
    81–82, 105n
Sozh River, 1
Stakhanov movement, 12
Stalin, I.V., 6, 9, 10, 13, 15,
    18, 54, 57, 117, 125
Stankevich, Jan, 16
State Chernobyl Committee, 28
State Committee for the Press, 119
State Defense Committee
    (USSR), 15, 16
Statute of the Duchy
    of Lithuania, 1
Stolypin, P., 9
Strategic Arms Reduction
    Treaty (START-1), 108
Stroyev, Yegor, 95
Stuart-Jervis, John, 78
Stupnikov, Aleksandr, 102, 119
Suslov, Mikhail, 22
Svaboda, 81–82

Tadzhikistan, 43, 63
Taiwan, 34
Tarnauski, H.S., 55, 67n
Tatars, 50
Tkachau, M., 48
Tovarishch, 102
Transcaucasian Republic, 6
Treaties of Paris, 3
Treaty of Brest-Litovsk (1918), 3
Treaty of Friendship and
    Cooperation, 111
Treaty of Riga (1921), 3, 6
Tsentral'naya Irmina coal
    mine, 12
Tsepkalo, Valery, 102

Tsesavets, Mikhail, 74
Tsikhinya, Valery, 79,
    91–92, 99
Tuleyev, Aman, 114
Turau-Pinsk (region), 1
Turevich, Art, 67n
Turkmenistan, 43
Twentieth Party Congress
    (CPSU), 19,
Twenty-Fifth Party
    Congress (CPSU), 21, 26n

Udmurts, 50
Ukraine, Ukrainians, 6, 7,
    18, 27–28, 42–43, 50,
    58–60, 63–64, 69, 107–109,
    120, 124, 126
Ukrainian National Association/
    Intra-Party Assembly
    (UNA-UNSO), 83, 114
unemployment, 39–40
Uniate (Greek Catholic Church), 1
Union of Afghan Veterans, 62
Union for the Liberation of
    Ukraine, 8
Union of Lublin (1569), 1
Union of Officers, 71
Union of Peasants and Workers, 7–8
Union of Soviet Socialist
    Republics (USSR), 6, 77
    dissolution of, 73
USSR Supreme Soviet, 13
United Civic Party, 79–80, 90, 125
United Jewish Socialist Party, 4
United Nations, 18, 28
United States (Americans), 34,
    43, 78, 90, 101–102, 109,
    120, 124
Urban, Michael, 49
urbanization, 50
Uzbekistan, 43

Vakar, Nicholas P., 6

Vecherniy Minsk, 82
Vershinin, K.A., 18
VGTRK (Moscow), 116
Vietnam, 120
Vileyka, 111
Vilna (Vilnius), 1, 2, 3,
    5, 14, 16, 48, 49
Vinnikava, Tamara, 37,
    80, 100, 105n
Vitsebsk (city), 2
Vitsebsk (oblast), 1, 6, 29, 31
Vladimir (ruler of Kievan Rus'), 1

wages, 36
Walesa, Lech, 110
Western Belarus, 12–15, 18
Western Ukraine, 13
Willoughby, Christopher, 36

Yakutou, Uladzimir, 21
Yalowitz, Kenneth, 102, 124

Yeltsin, Boris, 61, 72, 93,
    95, 107, 109–113,
    115, 117, 119
Yermachenka, I., 16
Yiddish, 2
Yugoslavia, 3, 110

Zaharodnik, I.Kh., 56–57
Zamyatalin, Uladzimir, 77, 92
Zaprudnik, Jan, 49
Zaruby (Vitsebsk Oblast), 33
Zavadesky, Dmitry, 118
Zelyony Luh, 56
"Zhdanovshchina," 18
Zhirinovsky, Vladimir,
    71, 118
Zhukov, G.K., 18
Zhylunovich, D., 5
Znavets, Pavel, 83
Zvyazda, 5, 79
Zyuganov, Gennadiy, 107, 118

5873